ANTIPASTI

ANTIPASTI

More than 80 Delicious Recipes for Wonderful Appetizers, Small Plates and More

A Fireside Book
Published by Simon & Schuster
New York   London   Toronto   Sydney

Fireside
A Division of Simon & Schuster, Inc.
1230 Avenue of the Americas
New York, NY 10020

First Fireside hardcover edition December 2008

Fireside and colophon are registered trademarks of Simon & Schuster, Inc.

For information about special discounts for bulk purchases,
please contact Simon & Schuster Special Sales
at 1-800-456-6798 or business@simonandschuster.com

Manufactured in China

10   9   8   7   6   5   4   3   2   1

ISBN-13: 978-1-4165-9348-5
ISBN-10:   1-4165-9348-9

Contents

ANTIPASTI

Contents

Introduction

THE ANTIPASTI

Customarily served before dinner, as their name suggests—"anti" (before) and "pasto" (meal)—antipasti are a cook's most eclectic offering. They may be served with cocktails or apéritifs, they can be a worthy substitute for a first or second course or for a fresh-vegetable side dish, and they may be combined to create a complete meal all on their own. A cocktail party or standing buffet supper requires small and easy-to-eat antipasti that can be picked up directly from the serving platter. Some know them as finger food; others call them tapas or amuse-bouche. Whatever name they go by, the concept remains the same: canapés, bite-sized quiches, appetizers, or tiny meatballs that we can "scoop up" with our own hands. Antipasti may feature meat or fish or may be vegetarian. They may be created with cooked or raw ingredients. They may be served hot or cold. The choices offered in this book are nearly endless. Just one word of advice: Antipasti should always be the lightest course on the menu. Begin by serving more delicate dishes and move on to those with a more decisive personality, building flavors and intensity to a crescendo.

ANTIPASTI: A LONG TRADITION

Antipasti have a long gastronomic tradition. In the banquets of ancient Rome, meals were preceded by light, appetizing dishes called gustio or gustatio. These were accompanied by mulsum, a drink made from wine and honey. Eggs, served hard-boiled, were a customary offering. Over time, the order in which the

antipasti course was served has shifted, but today it is most common to serve antipasti before the soup course. In Italian gastronomy, antipasti have been scaled down significantly, even at formal meals, and now generally appear as no more than two courses. The antipasti par excellence are naturally those based upon Italian smoked and cured meats. Dry-cured Parma ham and Zibello culatello are essential ingredients. If the meats are on the "sweet" side, they combine especially well with bread baked with salt; if, on the other hand, they are more savory and highly seasoned, they require a bread with a more neutral taste such as Tuscan bread, which is traditionally baked without the addition of salt to the dough. If possible, use a hand or manual slicer: The high speed of electric slicers melts the fat on the meat, which should melt in one's mouth instead. Seafood-based antipasti are also extremely popular: from traditional smoked salmon served on buttered toast to anchovies, from seafood salad to raw-fish carpaccio. Italy's twenty regions naturally lend their specialty dishes to the array of antipasti, including, for example, Sicily's panelle (fried chickpea-flour fritters), and arancini (fried balls of flavoured rice); the Piedmont's bagna càuda, a unique kind of fondue; deep fried "Ascolane" olives, typical of Ascoli Piceno in the Marche; or toasted bread (crostini) spread with the Tuscan version of chopped liver. In some countries, antipasti continue to occupy a position of importance in the wide variety of dishes served at dinner or other meals—if they don't literally overshadow

them. In Scandinavian countries, for example, and in Sweden in particular, the smörgåsbord (literally, the bread table) becomes an entire meal. It begins with fish and shellfish, moves on to smoked or dry-cured meats and sausages, and finishes with hot dishes. In every phase, the smörgåsbord is accompanied by breads of various kinds, including the classic rye cracker, by salads, and by high-proof alcoholic beverages.

The best-known antipasti, of course, are the Russian zakuski, which include pierogi (beignets or filled dumplings), caviar and other fish roe, morsels of rye bread with sauerkraut and smoked goose, salads of beets and potatoes, and varieties of smoked or marinated fish. The meze, originally Lebanese in origin but now common throughout the Middle East, represent yet another celebrated culinary tradition. More than a tradition, in fact, they very nearly reflect a way of approaching life itself. The presentation of meze involves a series of small dishes (from a minimum of four to as many as forty or so), accompanied by arak, a drink made of distilled anise seed and diluted with water and ice. The most common meze include purées made of chickpeas (humus) or sesame seeds (tahini); small balls of dough made from dried fava beans or chickpeas (falafel); grape leaves stuffed with rice (dolmas); fried dumplings filled with meat or cheese; a fish-roe dip (taramosalata); or a cream of garlic, yogurt, and cucumbers known as tzatziki in Greece and cacık in Turkey. The serving of the meze represents an important occasion for camaraderie and socializing and can last for many hours.

PRESENTATION

The antipasti are the first course to come to the table and, as such, they prepare the appetite for what is to follow. But the role of the antipasti isn't solely culinary—its colors should attract the attention, its aromas must be seductive, and its flavors should stimulate the imagination. As a result, the preparation of antipasti requires the same care that is devoted to the main dishes. A fundamental rule is that antipasti should be presented in small, inviting portions that are a feast, first and foremost, for the eyes. It is generally considered proper to serve antipasti on small plates that can be filled easily, giving the impression of abundance. Similarly, tarts, puffs, open-faced canapés, and the like should be arrayed on separate trays, from which they can be taken directly with the hands. Olives should be served in a bowl with a spoon, while sardines and caviar are served on a plate with a caviar knife or sardine fork. Pâté, on the other hand, should be presented on a plate with a pâté knife or similar instrument. Molds and timbales are more spectacular if they are plated in single-serving portions and enhanced by decorative garnishes (such as vegetables or fines herbs) and accompanied by a colourful and aromatic sauce. Creams, purées, and pâtés become irresistibly inviting if they are offered in fluffy mounds or dollops created with a pastry bag or arranged in pastry cups or barquettes of fruit and vegetables. With regard to the presentation of cold cuts, hard sausages, and salamis, and smoked and cured meats in general, remember that sliced meats lend themselves well to being wrapped around cut vegetables or thin bread sticks and can also be filled with a wide variety of ingredients. Antipasti prove to be quite practical dishes as well because the vast majority of them can be prepared in advance. Terrines and pâtés are even more flavorful if they are made a day ahead of time. The same is true of cream-based preparations and sauces, though these should be removed from the refrigerator at least a half-hour before serving. Finally, savory meat or vegetable pies and tarts, quiches, pasties, and the like can easily be reheated a few minutes before they are to appear on the table.

PASTRY CRUSTS: THE FUNDAMENTALS

Pasta Sfoglia: Puff Pastry

Puff pastry dough is the literal "base" of many recipes. It is extremely light and flaky and can be used in a multitude of dishes, both sweet and savory.

Ingredients

1 ½ cups (200 g) all-purpose flour
2 ¼ sticks (250 g) margarine
⅓ cup (100 ml) water
a generous pinch of salt

1. Mound the flour on your work surface and

place the water and the salt in its center. When the dough has achieved the proper consistency, wrap it in a dish towel and set aside for about twenty minutes.

2. Roll out the dough to a thickness of about ¼ inch (5 mm) and form it into a square. At the center, place the margarine sliced thinly. Fold the edges of the dough square inward, closing them completely as if creating a "package." Pass the rolling pin over the surface lightly, wrap the dough in aluminium foil, and place in the refrigerator for five minutes.

3. Now you are ready to begin the first pass. Return the dough to your work surface and, rolling it in a single direction only, create a rectangle approximately ½ inch (1 cm) thick. Fold the dough in on itself in three parts (fold ⅓ of the dough toward the center and then cover with the remaining flap) in order to create a quadrangle with three layers. Turn the dough ninety degrees.

4. For the second pass, roll the dough out once again, working in the same direction. Fold it once again in three sections, wrap in aluminium foil, and store for approximately thirty minutes in the refrigerator. Repeat these two steps an additional two times, for a total of six passes.

5. After completing the final pass, let the dough rest for at least an hour in the refrigerator before using it.

Chef's Secrets

A fundamental rule for creating a professional-quality pastry dough is to make sure that all the ingredients are at the same temperature and, thus, blend perfectly together. In particular, the margarine must have the same consistency as the dough: If it is too hard, it may break the dough; if, on the other hand, it is too soft, it may leak out the sides. Don't substitute butter for margarine. Butter contains very little water and, unlike margarine, will not release the steam that is necessary to cause the layers of flour to swell during cooking and add volume to the dough. Remember to make small holes in the dough so that steam will escape during cooking; otherwise, the dough will become soggy. If you want to give crusts a golden appearance, brush them with lightly beaten egg or with milk before baking.

Use in the Kitchen:

Pâte feuilletée or puff pastry is extremely versatile and lends itself to a wide variety of preparations both sweet and savoury.

For our purposes, puff pastry is best for creating small horns, tubes, or other pastry containers to hold mousses, creams, or pâtés; for vol-au-vents, bite-sized dumplings, or pasties with vegetable

and béchamel sauce fillings; as a wrapping for savoury strudels or baked vegetable cakes; or simply spread flat, seasoned, and cooked alone to create flaky, crunchy pastry squares.

Pasta Brisée: Brisée or Shortcrust Pastry Dough

Ingredients

2 ½ cups (300 g) all-purpose flour
⅔ stick (70 g) butter
1 egg
1 Tbsp extra-virgin olive oil
salt

1. Mound the flour and salt on your work surface. In the centre, break an egg. Add oil, salt, and warm water.
2. Work the dough, which will be fairly soft and stretchy, then wrap in plastic wrap and allow to stand in the refrigerator.

Chef's Secrets

It is essential to use butter and eggs that have been brought to room temperature and to work the dough quickly. Otherwise, the butter overheats

and may yield a dough that is insufficiently elastic. No less important: Let the dough stand in the refrigerator for at least thirty minutes to allow the various elements to "settle" and combine with one another. If you use brisée dough to create "savory" pies or tarts, remember to use a fork to pierce the bottom crust so that the dough does not rise during cooking and ruin the dish. Brisée dough may be kept in the refrigerator for a few days, wrapped in aluminium foil. It may also be frozen; defrost the dough slowly prior to use.

Use in the Kitchen:

Brisée dough is simply a pastry crust to which salt has been added. As a result, it is used principally as a base for vegetable and other savory pies; for pastry cups, barquettes, and small dumplings; and for various stuffed morsels that are brushed with beaten egg or milk and baked. Brisée dough can be accented with a dusting of poppy or sesame seeds or the like to add crunch and color.

Savoury Cannoncini -"Cannon Barrels"

The recipe that follows will allow you to create simple, savory cannoncini, which can then be filled with dozens of imaginative ingredients.

1. Roll out the brisée dough on your work surface.

2. Using a smooth pastry cutter or a sharp knife, cut out strips that are the same width as the stainless-steel cylinders or forms that you will use for shaping the cannoncini.

3. Wind the strips of dough around the tubular forms, leaving about an inch free for closing the cannoncini. Brush the unrolled edge of the dough with a small amount of beaten egg white and seal the cannoncini well.

4. Fry in hot oil (sunflower or other light vegetable oil) and drain carefully on absorbent paper.

Chef's Secrets

As soon as you remove the dough from the plastic wrap, begin working it immediately so the exterior will not dry out and crumble. Alternatively, protect the dough by covering it with a slightly dampened cloth. Phyllo dough may be used for baked appetizers as well as for creating very thin and crunchy triangles, purses, and pastry cups

perfect for accompanying a mousse of vegetables and fresh cheese.

Use in the Kitchen:

Fill the cannon-barrel-shaped "cannoncini" with a mixture of ricotta, olive oil, oregano, salt, and pepper and add a teaspoon of seedless diced tomato in the center. Or fill with white fish, such as grouper or cod, flavored with fines herbs and lemon peel.

SAUCES

Sauces and mousses are perfect for filling open-faced tartines, bruschetta, and savoury beignets or as an accompaniment to fresh crudités. The "basic" sauces that we describe here will prove to be invaluable allies in the creation of antipasti, adding flavor and fun to your creations.

Ricotta Cream with Ginger and Chives

Ingredients

¾ cup (200 g) ricotta, very fresh
fresh chives
1 Tbsp (20 g) ginger root, raw
1 Tbsp extra-virgin olive oil
salt and pepper

1. Strain the ricotta and work with a spatula to create a smooth cream. Season with olive oil, salt, and pepper.

2. Grate the ginger root and squeeze the pulp

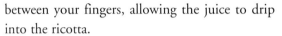

between your fingers, allowing the juice to drip into the ricotta.

3. Add the chopped chives and let the mousse absorb flavor for one hour in the refrigerator.

Yogurt Cream

Ingredients
2 Tbsp fresh chopped herbs (parsley, dill, oregano, basil)
1 ⅔ cups (400 g) Greek yogurt
2 cloves garlic
2 Tbsp honey
1 tsp salt
black pepper

1. Mix the ingredients in a bowl, then strain the mixture through a sieve. Allow to stand overnight in the refrigerator.

2. Serve the yogurt cream with mixed crudités.

Salmon Cream

Ingredients
¼ lb (80 g) smoked salmon
1 white onion
¾ cup (200 g) robiola cheese, fresh

½ tsp paprika
salt

1. Chop the onion and the salmon finely, blend with the robiola, dress with paprika, and season with salt.

2. Allow the salmon cream to stand in the refrigerator for one hour, then use to fill bite-sized tarts or vol-au-vents.

Prosciutto Mousse

Ingredients
1 lb (450 g) cooked ham
⅔ stick (70 g) butter
½ cup milk
2 Tbsp (20 g) all-purpose flour
¾ cup (200 ml) cream, fresh
nutmeg
salt and pepper

1. Cut the ham into small cubes or strips and pulse in a food processor.

2. In a small sauté pan, melt about 1/3 of the butter. Remove from heat and add the flour. Continue mixing and return to heat.

3. Add the milk and boil for three minutes. Season with salt and pepper and sprinkle with the nutmeg.

4. Add the ham to the resulting béchamel

sauce and strain through a sieve. Beat the cream, froth the rest of the butter, and incorporate these two ingredients into the ham cream.

5. Allow the ham mousse to stand for three to four hours in the refrigerator in a buttered mold.

This mousse, with its delicate flavor, can be served with crackers or your favorite bread, even a spiced or herbed variety.

Mustard Mayonnaise

Ingredients
1 egg yolk
1 Tbsp sweet mustard
8 Tbsp sunflower or other light vegetable oil
1 Tbsp extra-virgin olive oil
1 Tbsp balsamic vinegar
salt and pepper

1. Beat the egg yolk and the sweet mustard in a mixing bowl. Add the balsamic vinegar, blending slowly.

2. Add a drizzle of sunflower or other vegetable oil and then the olive oil, being careful to stir continuously so the mayonnaise will not separate.

3. Season with salt and pepper.

This sauce is an ideal accompaniment for crudités. In addition, it is an excellent alternative to butter when making toast-based tartines or canapés with smoked fish.

Hollandaise Sauce

Ingredients
2 egg yolks
¾ stick (100 g) butter
1 Tbsp all-purpose flour
1 Tbsp broth
½ cup vinegar
salt and pepper

1. Boil the vinegar, add salt and pepper, and allow the liquid to reduce to one-third of its volume. As soon as it has cooled, add the tablespoon of broth, the egg yolks, and about ⅔ of the butter, broken into pieces.

2. In a small pan set into a double boiler, beat the mixture with a French whip. Blend well, adding the rest of the butter and a little cold water as you do so. If desired, strain the sauce through a sieve to eliminate any lumps. Keep it in the double boiler until you are ready to serve.

Meat-Based Antipasti

Garlic Pastry Squares
with Porcini Mushrooms and Pancetta Ham

Serves 4

For the puff pastry:
1 ¼ cups (160 g) all-purpose flour
⅓ cup (80 ml) water
1 ⅔ sticks (200 g) margarine
salt

For the filling:
16 slices of pancetta ham, rolled
4 porcini mushrooms
1 shallot
1 clove garlic
2 Tbsp Béchamel sauce
1 Tbsp extra-virgin olive oil
¼ cup white wine, dry
1 small bunch parsley
salt and pepper

Preparation time: 20 minutes
Cooking time: 15 minutes
Difficulty: Easy
Calories: 624
Wine: Lambrusco dei Colli
di Parma

Prepare a lightly salted puff pastry dough (for directions, see p. 10). Extend the dough with a rolling pin (Picture 1) and cut out squares of approximately 3-4 inches (8-10 cm) on a side. Place the squares in a 425°F (220°C) oven and bake until the dough has turned a light golden-brown color.

1. Peel the shallot and garlic and mince together. Brown in extra-virgin olive oil. Wash the porcini mushrooms under running water, dry carefully with a paper towel, and slice thinly. Add to the shallot and garlic. Flavor with the white wine and cook (if additional liquid is necessary, add vegetable broth). Add salt and pepper to taste and add the béchamel.

2. Decorate the plates by alternating a square of pastry with a tablespoon of mushrooms and two slices of pancetta ham (heated for ten seconds in the microwave set on high or in a small, non-stick pan without oil until the pancetta ham crisps). Continue layering in this way, finishing with a layer of pastry and a tablespoon of mushrooms.

3. Dust with a pinch of chopped parsley and serve hot.

Foie Gras with Caramelized Tangerines,
Guanciale, and Red Onions

Serves 4

For the foie gras:
½ lb (200 g) foie gras
2 thin slices Guanciale

For the tangerines:
10 tangerine wedges
2 Tbsp sugar
2 pats butter

For the onion:
1 red onion
peanut oil

For the bread:
4 cups (500 g) all-purpose flour
4 cups (500 g) Manitoba flour
1 packet brewer's yeast
2 pats butter
1 generous Tbsp. (20 g) salt

Caramelize the tangerine wedges in a pan with the sugar and the butter (Picture 1).

1. Clean the red onion and slice thinly. Coat the onion in flour (Picture 2), shake to remove any excess, and fry in abundant oil (use peanut oil, sunflower oil, or other light vegetable oil).

2. In a small, non-stick pan, cook the of foie gras (Picture 3) and finish in a hot oven for a few minutes.

3. Prepare the bread by mixing together the white and the Manitoba flour, the yeast, the butter, and the salt. Allow the dough to rise for approximately two hours. Bake in a loaf pan at 350°F (170°C) until it is golden-brown. Slice, remove crusts, and heat in the oven until the bread is crunchy.

4. Assemble the plate in the following order: bread, tangerines, foie gras, guanciale, and red onions.

Interesting to Know: Manitoba flour is obtained from the milling of varieties of "soft" wheat grown in North America and originally cultivated in the Canadian province of Manitoba. Bread made with Manitoba flour has a significant absorption rate (up to 80% of its weight).

Preparation time: 35 minutes
Cooking time: 20 minutes
Difficulty: Medium
Calories: 758
Wine: Sagrantino di Montefalco

Pork Fritters
with Porcini Mushroom Salad

Serves 8

For the fritters:
1 cup (125 g) all-purpose flour
1 egg
1 cup (250 ml) milk
salt

For the filling:
½ lb (250 g) suckling pig, deboned
½ stick (60 g) butter
3-4 Tbsp (50 ml) milk
vegetable broth
¼ onion
1 clove garlic
marjoram, sage, bay leaf, chives
salt and pepper

For the sauce:
⅔ cup (150 ml) red vermouth
2 pats butter
2 bay leaves
3 Tbsp (30 g) rose hip compote

For the salad:
stale white bread
3 cups (200 g) Porcini mushrooms

Preparation time: 20 minutes
Cooking time: 25 minutes
Difficulty: Medium
Calories: 385
Wine: Carso Terrano

Mix together all the ingredients indicated for the fritters in order to obtain a batter that is homogenous, smooth, and without lumps. Fry the fritters, being careful not to overcook (Picture 1).

1. Brown the onion, the garlic, and the spices using only half the butter. Cut the meat into small pieces, add to the onion and garlic, and sauté (Picture 2). Pour in the broth and cook for approximately fifteen minutes. Finally, add the milk, the rest of the butter, the salt, and the pepper. Pulse the mixture in a food processor.

2. Spread the resulting pâté over the fritters (Picture 3), roll them, and allow them to cool completely. Brown the bay leaves and the rose hip compote in the butter, deglaze with the vermouth, and boil for a moment. Allow to cool.

3. Cut the pâté-filled fritters, now cooled, into very thin slices (no more than about ⅛ inch or 3-4 mm) and serve over a crunchy salad made of stale bread and porcini mushrooms cut into matchsticks and spiced with fines herbs and sprouts. Dress with the rose hip compote and vermouth mixture.

Escargot Skewers
with Potato Purée and Green Salsa

Serves 6

For the skewers:
6 dozen escargot
4 sprigs mint
2 cloves garlic
2 white onions
2 potatoes
4 slices Lardo di Colonnata
3 pats butter
2 Tbsp white vinegar
1 ⅔ cups (100 g) parsley
6 Tbsp (50 g) Pantelleria capers
¼ cup white wine
2 salt-preserved anchovies
1 egg, hard-boiled
¾ cup (200 ml) extra-virgin olive oil
⅔ cup (150 ml) milk
salt

Garnish:
1 tomato

Preparation time: 40 minutes
Cooking time: 30 minutes
Difficulty: Easy
Calories: 585
Wine: Gambellara

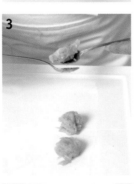

Mince half the Lardo di Colonnata together with the mint and the garlic. Brown in a pan (Picture 1) and add the snails (previously boiled and removed from their shells). Heat for a few minutes, allowing the flavors to combine, and add the wine.

1. Boil the potatoes and combine with the butter and the milk to obtain a purée. Season lightly with salt.

2. Slice the onions thinly and simmer them with the rest of the Lardo di Colonnata cut into small cubes. If necessary, add a small amount of water.

3. Place the fresh parsley, the anchovies, the hard-boiled egg, the vinegar, the capers, and a small amount of oil into a food processor with a glass container. Pulse together to make the green salsa. Create small skewers by placing four escargot on a toothpick (Picture 2) and bake for five minutes at 350°F (180°C).

4. Place three small spoonfuls of mashed potatoes (Picture 3) and an equal number of spoonfuls of the onion mixture on a serving plate, and arrange the skewers among them (Picture 4).

5. Dribble a few drops of the green salsa on the plate and garnish with the tomatoes, cut into small cubes, and a drizzle of extra-virgin olive oil.

Goose Breast
with Turnips and Beets

Serves 4

For the marinade:
1 goose breast, goose skin
½ cup (60 g) mixed vegetables, chopped
1 Tbsp (10 ml) gin
10 bay leaves
10 juniper berries
3 generous Tbsp (60 g) marine salt
black peppercorns
⅓ cup (30 g) cane sugar
vinegar

Vinaigrette for the white turnips:
2 turnips, medium
sugar
1 shallot
apple cider vinegar
6 Tbsp extra-virgin olive oil
salt and pepper

Vinaigrette for the beets:
2 beets, precooked
1 shallot
mustard
⅓ cup (100 ml) balsamic vinegar
6 Tbsp extra-virgin olive oil
3 Tbsp apple cider vinegar
salt and sugar

Preparation time: 40 minutes
Cooking time: 25 minutes
Difficulty: Medium
Calories: 570
Wine: Colli Morenici
del Garda Rosato

Tie the goose breast in such a way that the two skinless parts touch (Picture 1). Make incisions on the fat side and marinate the breast for approximately twenty-four hours in a bowl with the salt, the vinegar, the spices, and the rest of the ingredients listed for the marinade (Picture 2).

1. Drain the breast, wash, and dry carefully. Wrap the goose breast in plastic wrap (Picture 3) and chill.

2. Boil the turnips, sliced thinly, in salted water and then cool under running water. Slice the beets. Dress each with its own vinaigrette.

3. Cut the goose skin into small cubes and toss in a sauté pan to release the fat. Drain on paper towels and season with salt. Remove the goose breast from the refrigerator, making sure it has become quite firm, and cut into very thin slices.

4. Layer slices of goose breast with slices of turnips and beets. Dress with the mustard.

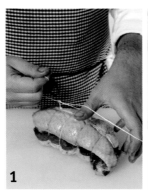

1   2   3

Mini-Strudels
with Pears and Cheese

Serves 6

For the strudel:
½ lb (250 g) phyllo dough
20 thin slices rolled pancetta ham
½ cup (50 g) walnuts, shelled
⅔ cup (60 g) parmesan cheese
2 Decana pears
2 Tbsp extra-virgin olive oil
1 pat butter
fennel seeds
salt and pepper

Roll out the phyllo dough on your work surface, cover it with overlapping slices of pancetta ham (preferably not aged). Finally, add the nuts chopped coarsely with a knife.

1. Peel the pears, cut them into fairly thin slices (Picture 1), and arrange over the strudel. Dust with shaved cheese, salt, and pepper.

2. Dress with a drizzle of extra-virgin olive oil and roll the dough onto itself, sealing the open edges carefully to make sure they do not open. Brush the strudel with the melted butter and sprinkle thoroughly with fennel seeds.

3. Bake the mini-strudels at 350°F (180°C) for approximately twenty minutes. Allow to cool and serve.

Kitchen tip: To create an alternate version of this strudel, use phyllo or puff pastry dough as a base and fill with a mixture made up of about ½ lb (200 g) of fresh salmon, four tablespoons of extra-virgin olive oil, chives, lemon thyme, and salt. Seal the strudel as indicated above, and bake at 375°F (190°C) for twenty minutes.

Preparation time: 15 minutes
Cooking time: 20 minutes
Difficulty: Easy
Calories: 445
Wine: Metodo Talento Trentino

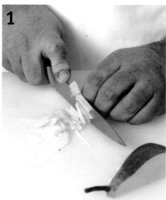

Belgian Endive
and Prosciutto Tarts

Serves 4

For the tarts:
1 cup (125 g) all-purpose flour
¾ stick (85 g) butter
2 Tbsp water
salt

For the filling:
2 heads Belgian endive
2 eggs
⅔ cup milk
1 Tbsp potato starch
½ clove garlic
2 pats butter
salt and pepper

Garnish:
⅕ lb (80 g) Parma ham

Prepare the dough with the flour, the softened butter, the salt, and the water, mixing the ingredients quickly. When the dough is smooth, form a ball, wrap it in plastic wrap, and set it aside in the refrigerator.

1. Blanch the endive in water and salt, drain, and dry with a dish towel. In a pan, melt the butter and sauté one-half of a clove of garlic. Remove the garlic and braise the endive for five minutes, seasoning with salt and pepper.

2. In a bowl, mix the eggs and the milk, along with the potato starch and a pinch of salt, and beat well (Picture 1). Remove the dough from the refrigerator and roll out to a thickness of about ¼ inch (½ cm).

3. Cut out four discs of dough of about 5 inches (12 cm) each in diameter. Butter and flour four small, single-serving molds and line them with the dough. Poke holes in the dough with a fork, arrange the braised endive in the molds, and cover with the egg mixture. Bake in a preheated 350°F (180°C) oven for twenty minutes.

4. As soon as the tarts have finished baking, remove them from the molds and arrange two or three thin slices of Parma ham over each.

Preparation time: 35 minutes
Cooking time: 20 minutes
Difficulty: Medium
Calories: 342
Wine: Tocai Friulano

Chicken Terrine
with a Balsamic Vinegar Infusion

Serves 8

For the terrine:
1 Chicken (whole)
2 egg yolks
⅔ cup (150 g) cream
6 Tbsp extra-virgin olive oil
1 potato
1 carrot
1 single stalk celery
1 tomato
1 onion
2 gelatin leaves
⅓ cup (100 ml) balsamic vinegar
poppy seeds
sesame seeds

Peel the tomato and dry the skin in the oven for twenty-five minutes at 250°F (120°C).

1. Prepare the broth with the tomato, the carrot, the celery, the onion, and the potato. As soon as the broth is ready, cut the hen into two parts, place it in the broth, and cook for at least forty minutes.

2. Remove the chicken meat from the bones and place in a cutter mixer along with the egg yolk, cream, extra-virgin olive oil, and potato (which has been boiled). Add a small amount of the broth, then turn the mixture into a terrine or soufflé mold lined with plastic wrap.

3. Allow the broth to reduce considerably. Filter out approximately ⅓ cup (100 ml), add the vinegar and the gelatin, which has been softened and then squeezed to remove excess liquid (Picture 1).

4. Pour the balsamic vinegar-flavored gelatin over the terrine to the edge of the mold and let stand in the refrigerator for approximately one hour.

5. When you are ready to serve, unmold the terrine and pass through a mixture of poppy and sesame seeds. Cut into slices and decorate with petals of tomato skin.

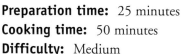

Preparation time: 25 minutes
Cooking time: 50 minutes
Difficulty: Medium
Calories: 428
Wine: Verdicchio di Matelica

Pâté de Foie Gras
with Frothy Vov Mousse

Serves 4

For the pâté:
4 slices (90 g each) fatty goose liver
½ Tbsp balsamic vinegar
½ cup (50 g) Ginger root, sliced
¼ cup (20 g) sugar

For the mousse:
¾ cup (200 ml) Vov (egg liqueur)
4 egg whites
½ Tbsp balsamic vinegar

To prepare the ginger comfit, julienne the ginger root with a sharp knife and parboil for four minutes (Picture 1). Dry the sliced ginger and candy with the sugar until a syrup is formed.

1. Prepare the Vov mousse: Put the Vov, the egg whites, and a drop of balsamic vinegar into a seltzer bottle. Shake well and load the bottle with a double charge of CO_2. Immerge in a bain-marie to maintain its temperature.

2. Prepare a very hot iron skillet. Scald the liver on both sides (Picture 2) and then place the slices in a 400°F (200°C) oven for approximately five minutes.

3. Dry the liver on a paper towel and serve (Picture 3) accompanied by the frothy Vov mousse. Finish with a drop of balsamic vinegar.

Interesting to Know: The seltzer bottle is a hermetically closed container equipped with CO_2 cartridges (generally inserted into the lid of the bottle) that makes it possible to rapidly create whipped cream, mousses, and the like. It's a useful tool, though rarely used in the ordinary household kitchen.

Preparation time: 15 minutes
Cooking time: 30 minutes
Difficulty: Difficult
Calories: 325
Wine: Marsala Riserva

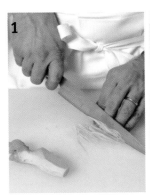

Broccoli Timbale
with Prosciutto Mousse

Serves 4

For the timbale:
3 (500 g) large potatoes
⅔ lb (300 g) broccoli
½ lb (250 g) cooked ham
½ cup (100 g) cream, fresh
6 Tbsp extra-virgin olive oil
salt and pepper

Garnish:
2 Tbsp black olive paste

Preparation time: 25 minutes
Cooking time: 15 minutes
Difficulty: Easy
Calories: 702
Wine: Velletri Bianco

Wash the potatoes and cook them in boiling water. In the meantime, boil the broccoli in salted water.

1. Cut the prosciutto cotto into pieces and pulse in a food processor. Add the cream (Picture 1) and mix carefully.

2. Drain the broccoli when it is slightly "al dente" (Picture 2), cream in the food processor, dress with oil and pepper and set aside.

3. Drain the potatoes, mash with a potato masher (Picture 3), and dress with extra-virgin olive oil, salt, and pepper.

4. In a timbale mold or ramekin, layer the prepared ingredients in the following order: first the potatoes, then the prosciutto mousse (Picture 4), and finally the broccoli.

5. Let the timbales stand in the refrigerator for one hour, then release them from the molds and dress the top layer of broccoli lightly with black olive paste.

Interesting to Know: Timbales take their name from the container in which they were traditionally cooked: a slightly conical mold similar to an ancient Arabic musical instrument, the thabal (a kind of drum). Originally, the timbale was formed in a pastry crust made of flour, butter, salt and water, or of flour with small amounts of sugar and spices added.

Zucchini, Pancetta Ham,
and Caprino Cheese Pie

Serves 4-6

For the shortcrust pastry dough:
1 ½ cup (200 g) all-purpose flour
¾ stick (100 g) butter
1 egg
1 Tbsp extra-virgin olive oil
salt

For the filling:
¾ lb (400 g) zucchini
1 cup (100 g) caprino cheese, fresh
12 thin slices pancetta ham
3 Tbsp extra-virgin olive oil
¼ cup (30 g) pine nuts
2 Tbsp parmesan cheese
4 eggs
¾ cup (200 ml) milk
½ cup (100 ml) cream, fresh
2 cloves garlic
salt and pepper

Preparation time: 20 minutes
Cooking time: 30 minutes
Difficulty: Easy
Calories: 621
Wine: Friuli Pinot Grigio

Prepare the briseé dough (see directions on p. 12), cover with plastic wrap, and allow to stand in a cool place for twenty minutes.

1. Cube the zucchini (Picture 1) and sauté in olive oil along with the smashed cloves of garlic. Brown until soft but do not allow to darken. Season with salt and pepper and set aside to cool.

2. In a mixing bowl, beat the eggs with the parmesan, the milk, the cream, and the finely chopped pancetta ham. Season with salt and pepper.

3. Eliminate the garlic and cream the zucchini in a food processor. At the end, add the caprino cheese cut into chunks and pulse again for a few seconds. Add the zucchini and caprino mixture to the eggs, cream, and pancetta ham and blend well.

4. Roll the brisée dough into a single, thin layer and line a 9-10-inch (24 cm) cake pan with the dough. Pour the mixture of zucchini and eggs over the dough. Sprinkle the pine nuts, which you have previously blanched in a pan (Picture 2), over the surface. Cut away any excess dough. Bake at 325°F (170°C) for twenty-five to thirty minutes, cut into slices, and serve.

1

Prosciutto Quiche
with Olives

Serves 6

For the olive cake:

½ lb (200 g) cooked ham in a single slice

1 ¼ cups (150 g) cake flour

⅕ lb (100 g) Gruyère

¼ cup (50 g) ricotta cheese

3 pats butter

5 Tbsp parmesan cheese

30 green olives, pitted

4 eggs

¼ cup white wine

½ packet yeast

salt and pepper

Preparation time: 15 minutes
Cooking time: 45 minutes
Difficulty: Easy
Calories: 270
Wine: Pomino Bianco

Work the ricotta and the butter together with a whisk to obtain an even cream without lumps (Picture 1).

1. Cut the prosciutto into small pieces after removing the fat. Slice the olives in half. Add them, along with the egg yolks (Picture 2), the wine, the sifted flour, the parmesan, the shaved Gruyère, salt, pepper, and the yeast to the butter and ricotta. (Picture 3).

2. Pour the mixture into a buttered and floured loaf pan and smooth the surface (Picture 4).

3. Bake in a 400°F (200°C) oven for forty-five minutes. Remove from the oven and set aside to cool. Cut the olive cake into slices that aren't too thick and serve, preferably warm.

Kitchen tip: In this recipe, robiola cheese can be substituted for ricotta. Don't forget, however, that the taste of robiola varies according to whether it is fresh or aged. Aged robiola brings with it stronger notes, sometimes with a decided pungency. Fresh robiola is best for this recipe, however; the flavor is delicate and not too insistent and the texture is velvety.

Beef Sausage
with Two-Mushroom Salad

Serves 4

For the beef sausage:
½ lb (200 g) beef sirloin or rump
⅕ lb (100 g) montasio cheese
⅓ cup (100 ml) white wine, dry
coriander seeds
cinnamon powder
salt and whole black peppercorns

For the salad:
⅕ lb (100 g) mixed salad greens
5 Tbsp extra-virgin olive oil
4 porcini mushrooms
2 cups (150 g) galletti mushrooms
2 Tbsp balsamic vinegar

Place a few peppercorns plus a small number of coriander seeds into a mortar and pulverize.

1. Place the meat in a bowl and dust with the mixture of ground coriander and pepper and with the cinnamon (Picture 1). Cover the spiced meat with the white wine and marinate for approximately one hour.

2. Mince the meat and cut the cheese into small cubes. Mix the two ingredients together well in a bowl (Picture 2).

3. Clean the galletti mushrooms and slice the porcinis. Blanch the gallettis, wash the salad greens, and toss both with the porcini mushrooms.

4. Wrap the meat in plastic wrap and form it into the shape of a large sausage (Picture 3). Place in the refrigerator for approximately ten minutes.

5. Cut the sausage into thick slices and serve with the two-mushroom salad dressed with extra-virgin olive oil and balsamic vinegar.

Kitchen tip: To give this recipe a slightly different character, use only porcini mushrooms or only gallettis in order to emphasize the flavour of one or the other.

Preparation time: 1 hour and 30 minutes
Cooking time: 5 minutes
Difficulty: Easy
Calories: 353
Wine: Lago di Caldaro Rosso

Belgian Endive Soufflé
with Prosciutto Cotto

Serves 6

For the soufflé:

1 ¼ lb (600 g) Belgian endive
½ stick (60 g) butter
⅓ cup (40 g) all-purpose flour
¾ cup (200 ml) milk
¼ lb (100 g) cooked ham
4 Tbsp parmesan cheese
3 eggs
1 shallot
nutmeg
salt and pepper

Wash the Belgian endive and cut into strips. In a pan, delicately melt half the butter, sauté the chopped shallot, and add the endive. Season with salt and cook for a few minutes, stirring occasionally. Add a half-cup of water, cover the pan, and cook over very low heat for ten minutes. Uncover and, over high heat, allow the liquid to evaporate. Set aside to cool.

1. In a second pan, melt the rest of the butter and incorporate the sifted flour, mixing constantly. Pour in the cold milk and bring to a boil.

2. Cook until the mixture thickens. Add salt and pepper, flavour with a dash of grated nutmeg and the grated parmesan, and mix. Cut the prosciutto into small cubes and add to the cheese mixture along with the cooked endive.

3. Incorporate the egg yolks one at a time, stirring constantly (Picture 1). Beat the egg whites until they peak and add them carefully to the mixture, folding delicately from the bottom of the pan toward the top. (Picture 2).

4. Butter a series of molds (Picture 3), fill them with the batter, and bake at 350°F (180°C) for about twenty minutes. Lower the temperature to 325°F (170°C) and cook for an additional ten minutes. Serve immediately

Preparation time: 20 minutes
Cooking time: 55 minutes
Difficulty: Easy
Calories: 237
Wine: Falerno del Massico Bianco

Rabbit Salad with Bacon,
Shoestring Potatoes, and Leek Cream

Serves 4

For the salad:
⅔ lb (300 g) saddle of rabbit
6 thin slices bacon
⅔ cup white wine
1 sprig rosemary
2 sage leaves
2 bay leaves
1 Tbsp all-purpose flour
4 Tbsp extra-virgin olive oil
1 clove garlic
2 sprigs thyme
salt and pepper

For the leek cream:
1 leek
2 pats butter
¼ cup white wine
⅔ cup (150 g) cream, fresh
salt and pepper

For the potatoes:
2 (250 g) medium potatoes
8 Tbsp sunflower or other light
vegetable oil

Preparation time: 30 minutes
Cooking time: 30 minutes
Difficulty: Medium
Calories: 472
Wine: Rosso di Montalcino

Debone the saddle of rabbit (Picture 1), dividing it into two parts. Lightly salt and pepper the interior. Roll and close the ends with toothpicks.

1. Cut the bacon into thin strips. Place the oil into a pan and brown the rosemary, the sage, the sprig of thyme, the bay leaf, and the clove of garlic (peeled and smashed). Lay the two rolled rabbit saddle pieces, lightly floured, into the pan along with the bacon (Picture 2). Lightly season with salt and pepper and brown the rabbit on all sides (Picture 3). Add the white wine. Cook, covered, for ten minutes over low heat

2. In the meantime, wash and cut the leeks into rounds. Brown them in butter and add the white wine. Pour in the cream and let the sauce thicken for five minutes. Lightly season with salt and pepper.

3. Peel the potatoes and cut them into shoestrings. Wash and dry them, then fry for approximately five minutes. Drain on a paper towel.

4. On serving dishes, create a bed of leek cream, arrange the rabbit, cut into mini-filets not more than ¼ inch (½ cm) in thickness, over the cream and garnish with the potatoes.

Country-Style Babà
with Prosciutto Cotto and Mozzarella

Serves 4

For the babà:

2 ½ cups (300 g) all-purpose flour
1 (150 g) medium potato
1 packet brewer's yeast
⅔ cup (150 ml) milk
3 Tbsp extra-virgin olive oil
⅓ lb (150 g) cooked ham
⅓ lb (150 g) mozzarella
salt

Preparation time: 20 minutes
Cooking time: 1 hour
Difficulty: Easy
Calories: 424
Wine: Trentino Moscato Rosa

Boil the potatoes in lightly salted water. When they are thoroughly cooked, drain, and set aside to cool. Dissolve the brewer's yeast in the warm milk.

1. Pour the flour into a bowl and add the potatoes, mashing them directly in the bowl with a potato ricer (Picture 1). Add the olive oil and season with salt. Add the yeast dissolved in the milk and the slightly beaten eggs. Begin working the mixture with the help of a whisk or a wooden spoon.

2. Cut the mozzarella and the prosciutto into small cubes and add both to the potato mixture (Pictures 2-3). Mix until all the ingredients are well blended. Butter and lightly flour a series of disposable timbale molds.

3. Fill the molds with the mixture, leaving approximately ½ inch (1 cm) of the border clear (Picture 4). Allow the babà to rise in a warm place for forty minutes. Preheat the oven to 350°F (180°C). When it is hot, bake the babà for twenty minutes. Remove from the oven, unmold, and serve immediately.

Brioche with Vegetable, Cheese, and Speck Filling

Serves 4

For the puff pastry:

1 ¼ cups (160 g) all-purpose flour

⅓ cup water

¾ cup (200 g) margarine

Salt

For the filling:

1 (100 g) large yellow bell pepper

½ cup (50 g) zucchini

1 (100 g) small potato

½ spring onion

⅔ cup (50 g) broccoli tops

2 medium slices Scamorza cheese

3-4 thin slices of speck

1 bunch parsley

1 clove garlic

3 Tbsp extra-virgin olive oil

1 egg

salt and pepper

Prepare the puff pastry dough according to the directions given on p. 10-11. Clean the peppers and the zucchini and cut into small cubes. Boil the potatoes and cube them as well. Boil the broccoli tops and cut them into small pieces. Heat the oil in a pan and brown the spring onion, the garlic, and the chopped parsley.

1. Add the rest of the vegetables and toss for three to four minutes over medium heat. Add salt and pepper and pour the filling into a bowl to cool. Add the scamorza and the speck cut into cubes.

2. Extend the pastry crust on your work surface and, using a pastry cutter, cut out eight triangular wedges of equal size. Brush the points of the wedges lightly with beaten egg. Place a teaspoon of filling at the base of each triangle.

3. Starting from the base of the triangle, roll carefully, pressing the filling toward the middle, until the rolls are completely closed (Pictures 1-2). Press at the edges, curve toward the interior (Picture 3), and place the brioche on a baking sheet lined with parchment or non-stick oven paper.

4. Brush the brioche with the beaten egg and bake in a 350°F (180°C) oven for twelve to fifteen minutes. Serve immediately.

Preparation time: 35 minutes
Cooking time: 20 minutes
Difficulty: Medium
Calories: 417
Wine: Alto Adige Sylvaner

Oven-Roasted
Radicchio Salad

Serves 4

For the salad:
1 lb (500 g) red radicchio
1 lb (400 g) mozzarella
⅓ lb (150 g) Parma ham
4 Tbsp extra-virgin olive oil
salt and pepper

Remove the stem ends from the radicchio leaves and wash carefully. Drain, dry, and cut the leaves lengthwise into slices about ¼ inch (½ cm) thick (Picture 1).

1. Dress the radicchio with extra-virgin olive oil, salt, and pepper. Heat a pan and cook the radicchio for around three minutes.

2. Heat the oven to 350°F (180°C). Place the radicchio into a ceramic oven-proof baking dish. Cut the mozzarella into slices and arrange over the radicchio (Picture 2).

3. Bake the radicchio and mozzarella in the oven for approximately six minutes. Arrange thin slices of prosciutto crudo over the radicchio and serve hot.

Interesting to Know: Two varieties of radicchio exist: early red radicchio and late red radicchio. In the first, the head is larger, elongated, and tightly closed; the leaves have a slightly bitter taste and a fairly crunchy texture. In the second, the appearance is of an enlarged bud, uniform and compact, with leaves that are closed and inward-curving. It is crunchy with a pleasantly bitter taste.

Preparation time: 10 minutes
Cooking time: 10 minutes
Difficulty: Easy
Calories: 386
Wine: Piave Tocai

Savory Prosciutto
Roll

Serves 4

For the potato dough:
½ lb (250 g) bread starter
2 cups (250 g) all-purpose flour
2 (250 g) medium potatoes
1 packet brewer's yeast
2 Tbsp extra-virgin olive oil
1 tsp lard
3 generous Tbsp (50 ml) water
1 generous Tbsp (20 g) salt

For the filling:
½ lb (200 g) cooked ham
½ lb (250 g) mozzarella

Preparation time: 30 minutes
Cooking time: 20 minutes
Difficulty: Medium
Calories: 841
Wine: Ortrugo

Boil the potatoes and mash them. Add them to the bread starter along with the water, the olive oil, the lard, and the salt. Work the dough, adding the yeast and the flour a little at a time. The resulting dough should be smooth and pliable.

1. Place the dough in a bowl, cut an "X" into the surface, and cover the bowl with plastic wrap. Allow the dough to rise for thirty minutes.

2. Roll out the dough with a rolling pin or else with the tips of the fingers onto a sheet of parchment or non-stick oven paper. Allow to rise for thirty minutes. Distribute the mozzarella, cut into cubes, over the dough (Picture 1) and cover with thin slices of prosciutto cotto (Picture 2).

3. Heat the oven to 400°F (200°C). Form the dough into a single, tight roll (Picture 3). Cut slices just over ½ inch (1.5 cm) thick (Picture 4) and arrange them on a non-stick cookie sheet or similar covered with parchment or non-stick oven paper. Bake for twenty minutes. Serve hot.

Interesting to Know: To prepare the bread starter, dissolve approx. ⅓ oz. (10 g) of yeast in about ⅔ cup (125 ml) of warm water. Add two cups (250 g) of all-purpose flour, 1 tablespoon extra-virgin olive oil, and a pinch of salt. Knead until you've obtained smooth, even dough. Allow to rise for about two hours before using.

Parsley and Pancetta Ham
Flat Bread

Serves 4

For the dough:
2 cups (250 g) all-purpose flour
1 packet brewer's yeast
⅓ cup water
salt

For the filling:
3 bunches parsley
¼ lb (100 g) pancetta ham
¼ lb (100 g) provola, smoked or semi-sharp
4 anchovy fillets, oil-preserved
1 medium onion
4 Tbsp extra-virgin olive oil
ground black pepper

Pour the flour into a bowl and add a pinch of salt. In a separate container, dissolve the yeast in warm water. When the yeast is dissolved, pour it onto the flour and blend until a smooth, soft dough results.

1. Work the dough with your hands. Form into a ball and place in a container covered with a dish towel. Allow to rise in a warm place for forty-five minutes.

2. Once the dough has risen, roll it into a circle about ¼ inch (½ cm) thick. Drizzle two tablespoons of extra-virgin olive oil over the dough, then arrange the thinly sliced onion, the pancetta ham cut into strips, the provola cut into small pieces, the anchovies broken into pieces, and the coarsely chopped parsley (Pictures 1-2).

3. Finish with a dusting of black pepper and a drizzle of the remaining olive oil. Pick up the lower edge of the dough and fold it toward the center to form a roll, pressing down gently (Picture 3).

4. Arrange the dough roll on a baking sheet lined with parchment or non-stick oven paper and turn the ends down to create a horseshoe shape. Bake in a preheated 350°F (180°C) oven for twenty-five minutes. Serve hot or cold.

Preparation time: 30 minutes
Cooking time: 25 minutes
Difficulty: Easy
Calories: 446
Wine: Falerno del Massico Bianco

1   2   3

Vegetable-Based Antipasti

Vegetable Caponata
with Thyme

Serves 4

For the caponata:

1 eggplant
½ red bell pepper
½ yellow bell pepper
1 zucchini
1 stalk celery
½ white onion
1 carrot
2 Tbsp extra-virgin olive oil
thyme
salt and pepper

Wash all the vegetables under running water and dry them well. Chop the onion coarsely and simmer slowly in a sauce pan with the extra-virgin olive oil.

1. Cut the bell peppers in half (Pictures 1-2) and remove seeds and internal strings or fibers. Cut them into cubes, add to the onion, and cook. Cut the celery and the carrot into small cubes and add to the other vegetables.

2. Divide the eggplant into four wedges and remove the seeds. Cut the eggplant into cubes and add to the vegetables already in the process of cooking. Season lightly with salt and pepper and cook, covered, for five minutes.

3. Cut the zucchini into small cubes and add it to the other vegetables when cooking is nearly complete. Season with the thyme leaves and serve the caponata in small bowls.

Kitchen tip: Substitute seasonal vegetables and/or your favorites, according to your preferences. A winter caponata, for example, might include artichokes, mixed mushrooms, squash, and carrots.

Preparation time: 15 minutes
Cooking time: 15 minutes
Difficulty: Easy
Calories: 89
Wine: Elba Bianco

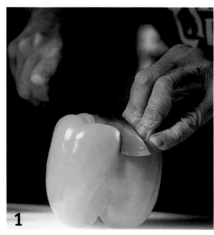

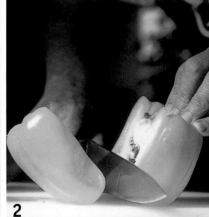

1

2

Eggplant Dumplings
in Cherry Tomato Sauce

Serves 4

For the bundles:
1 eggplant
1 shallot
½ hot pepper
6 Tbsp extra-virgin olive oil

For the crepes:
2 cups (500 ml) milk
2 eggs
1 ½ cups (200 g) all-purpose flour
salt and pepper

For the sauce:
½ lb (200g) cherry tomatoes, peeled
2 Tbsp extra-virgin olive oil
1 clove garlic
basil
salt and pepper

Preparation time: 25 minutes
Cooking time: 20 minutes
Difficulty: Easy
Calories: 388
Wine: Lugana

Pour the milk into a mixing bowl and beat in the eggs. Add the flour (Picture 1) and continue to blend with a whisk. Salt and set aside for twenty minutes.

1. Chop the shallot and sauté until golden in a sauce pan with two tablespoons of extra-virgin olive oil and the hot pepper, crumbled. Wash the eggplant, cut it into small pieces, and add to the shallot (Picture 2). Cook, covered. Season with salt and pepper, and then whip in a blender or food processor.

2. Place two tablespoons of oil into a small pan, smash the garlic into the oil and bring the oil to boil on a low heat. Add the tomato and let the mixture thicken, seasoning with the basil leaves.

3. Filter the crêpe batter through a strainer and pour a small amount into a non-stick pan greased with the rest of the oil (Picture 3), turning the pan to cook evenly. Cook for two minutes, then lift the border of the crêpe and flip to cook on the other side.

4. . Allow the crêpes to cool on a cloth and then spoon the eggplant cream into the center of each (Picture 4). Close the crêpes to form small dumplings, heat for five minutes in the oven, and serve over a puree of tomatoes creamed in a blender or food processor.

Tomato and Bread Mélange

Serves 4

For the mélange:
¾ lb (360 g) rustic Tuscan bread, stale
¾ cup (220 g) tomatoes, stewed (canned or bottled)
2 red tomatoes, ripe
1 bunch basil
1 clove garlic
8 Tbsp extra-virgin Tuscan olive oil
1 tsp agar, powdered
salt and pepper

Garnish:
basil

Preparation time: 25 minutes
Cooking time: 25 minutes
Difficulty: Medium
Calories: 453
Wine: Gavi di Rovereto

Mince the garlic and sauté in a pan with half the oil until golden. Then add the crushed tomatoes. Add salt and pepper and the julienned basil. Cook over low heat until the liquid is well absorbed. Remove from heat, add the bread cut into small cubes, and blend well until the bread is softened. Take care not to break up the cubes.

1. Pour the mixture into a rectangular mold or baking dish lined with parchment or non-stick oven paper. Spread evenly, cover with plastic wrap, and let stand in the refrigerator.

2. Blanch the whole tomatoes and peel them (Picture 1). Place them in a food processor with a glass bowl along with the remaining oil, a small amount of water, the basil, and salt and pepper. Process well. Strain the resulting mixture through a sieve (Picture 2) and heat. Soften the agar in cold water and then dissolve completely in water for five minutes (Picture 3). Allow to come to room temperature and then pour over the bread mixture

3. Place in the refrigerator for thirty minutes and then remove from the mold. Cut the mélange into squares and pass under the salamander grill (or oven broiler) to heat the surface. Serve with the julienned basil.

Interesting to Know: Agar is a gelatin obtained from seaweed and is used in the kitchen as a thickening agent.

Chickpea and Eggplant Pâté

Serves 4

For the pâté:

2 large eggplant
1 cup (200 g) chickpeas, dry
1 red bell pepper
1 yellow bell pepper
3 Tbsp sesame oil
3 Tbsp extra-virgin olive oil
1 small bunch parsley
4 medium slices bread for toasting
1 clove garlic
1 bay leaf
salt and pepper

Boil the chickpeas (after soaking them for twelve hours in cold water) with the bay leaf and the clove of garlic.

1. Peel the eggplant (Picture 1), slice lengthwise, and make parallel slits in the flesh with a knife at several points. Bake at 350°F (180°C) for approximately thirty minutes or until the eggplant is soft.

2. Using a spoon, extract the meat of the eggplant and whip in a food processor along with the cooked and drained chickpeas. Strain the resulting mixture through a sieve and place in a mixing bowl. Dress with the extra-virgin olive oil, the sesame oil, the chopped parsley, salt, and pepper. Set aside in a cool place.

3. Roast the bell peppers over a flame, place them in a tightly closed nylon sack, and allow them to sweat for twenty minutes. Peel, wash, and thinly julienne.

4. Arrange the eggplant and chickpea pâté in small terrines or individual serving bowls, garnish with the julienned bell peppers, and accompany with thin slices of bread toasted in a non-stick pan or under the broiler. Serve immediately.

Preparation time: 15 minutes
Cooking time: 30 minutes
Difficulty: Easy
Calories: 424
Wine: Lacryma Christi Bianco

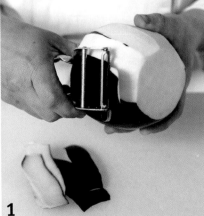

1

Burrata Cheese Molds
with Vegetables

Serves 4

For the burrata molds:

⅔ lb. (300 g) burrata cheese, fresh

2 baby carrots

1 heart of green celery

2 zucchini

6 Tbsp extra-virgin olive oil

4 medium slices bread for toasting

a handful string beans

thyme

salt and pepper

Boil the string beans in lightly salted water, drain, and allow to cool. Whip in a food processor with salt and with extra-virgin olive oil in order to obtain a thin cream.

1. Wash the zucchini and remove the ends. Julienne the zucchini and then cut them mirepoix fashion (a very fine dice). Clean the carrots and cut into small cubes (Pictures 1-2-3). Julienne the celery as well.

2. Blanch the vegetables in salted water for one minute and then chill them in a bowl of ice. Whip the burrata cheese in a mixer or food processor with a small amount of olive oil and the thyme. Blend in the vegetables, which have been carefully dried. Season with pepper.

3. Slice the bread thinly and toast under the broiler until it is golden-brown.

4. Fill a pastry cutter, tart ring, or similar with the burrata mixture and unmold on the serving dishes. Finish with the wafers of bread and the string bean cream.

Interesting to Know: Burrata cheese is a specialty of the south of Italy and is very similar to mozzarella. Both cheeses begin with the same basic mixture, in fact. Burrata, is then "frayed" and mixed with cream. Burrata has a sweet flavor and velvety texture.

Preparation time: 20 minutes

Cooking time: 10 minutes

Difficulty: Easy

Calories: 351

Wine: Verdicchio dei Castelli di Jesi

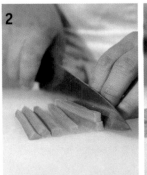

Mushroom Mille Feuille
with Sweet Pecorino

Serves 4

For the mille feuille:

½ lb (250 g) phyllo dough
½ lb (250 g) pecorino cheese, sweet
4 medium-large portobello mushrooms
1 lemon
4 Tbsp extra-virgin olive oil
1 pat butter
fresh milled black ground pepper
salt

Extend the phyllo dough on your work surface and cut out a number of squares of equal size. Arrange them on a non-stick baking sheet (or a baking pan lined with oiled paper).

1. Melt the butter and brush it onto the prepared squares. Salt and bake for eight minutes at 375°F (190°C).

2. In the meantime, clean the mushrooms carefully (they should be as firm as possible) with a damp paper towel. Slice them thinly.

3. Cut the pecorino into thin slices. Dress the mushrooms with salt, oil, and a small amount of lemon juice. Dust with pepper and layer the phyllo wafers with cheese and mushrooms. Serve warm.

Kitchen tip: This recipe recommends a "sweet," soft pecorino. In this case, that means avoiding aged or "sharp" pecorinos, which are often quite strong and which would overwhelm the delicate flavors of the mushrooms.

Preparation time: 20 minutes
Cooking time: 10 minutes
Difficulty: Easy
Calories: 490
Wine: Riesling Renano

Artichoke, Egg,
and Truffled Ricotta Casserole

Serves 4

For the artichokes:
14 small artichokes, mammola variety
1 lemon

For the filling:
4 eggs
1 shallot
2-3 drops truffle oil
1 Tbsp extra-virgin olive oil
1 cup (250 g) ricotta
2 Tbsp parmesan cheese
salt and pepper

Remove the tough outer leaves from the artichokes and use a corer to clean out the interior.

1. Place the artichokes in water adding the juice of half a lemon to keep them from turning black. Cook them in salted water for ten minutes until they are soft and compact.

2. Mix the ricotta with the shallot, chopped and simmered in a small amount of extra-virgin olive oil and water. Add the grated parmesan, the salt, the pepper, and the truffle oil.

3. Drain the artichokes, turn them upside down to eliminate remaining liquid. Stuff them with the ricotta mixture (Picture 1) and leave a concave space in the middle of each.

4. Grease an oven-proof baking dish with olive oil and arrange the artichokes in the bottom. Bake for fifteen minutes at 350°F (180°C). Remove from the oven and break the yolk of one egg in each artichoke (Picture 2). Return to the oven and bake for another five minutes at 350°F (180°C). The egg yolk should be warm but should not solidify. Serve the artichokes hot.

Interesting to Know: The mammola variety of artichoke is smaller than the more common version. Originally from Sardinia, it is a bright purple colour, has no spines, and is very tender and flavorful.

Preparation time: 35 minutes
Cooking time: 15 minutes
Difficulty: Easy
Calories: 280
Wine: Valdadige Pinot Grigio

1

2

Olive Pâté Tarts
with Caprino Cheese

Serves 4

For the tarts:
8 slices (for each tart) whole-wheat sandwich bread
¾ cup (200 g) black olive paste
¾ cup (200 g) green olive paste
1 ¼ cups (300 g) caprino cheese, fresh
3 Tbps extra-virgin olive oil
pepper

Garnish:
¾ cup (100 g) stuffed green olives

In a bowl, cream together the caprino cheese with the olive oil and a pinch of pepper (Picture 1).

1. Spread the green olive paste on two slices of bread and cover each with another slice of bread. Next, create a layer of caprino cheese and cover with another slice of bread.

2. Spread the black olive paste and cover with the last slice of bread.

3. Seal well in plastic wrap and place in the refrigerator to set for at least one hour.

4. Cut the bread into strips, triangles, or rectangles, and decorate each tart with a stuffed green olive, secured with a toothpick.

Kitchen tip: Here's an alternative version of this recipe. Mix ¾ cup (200 g) of caprino cheese (as fresh as possible) and ⅓ cup (100 g) of robiola. Or, for a slightly more pronounced flavor, use the same amount of sweet gorgonzola in place of the robiola, creaming the gorgonzola and the caprino together and spreading the cream on the tarts.

Preparation time: 10 minutes
Difficulty: Easy
Calories: 497
Wine: Fiano di Avellino

1

Mini-Pizzas
with Bell Peppers and Champignon Mushrooms

Serves 4

For the dough:
¾ cup (100 g) all-purpose flour
3 Tbsp (50 ml) water
½ cup (125 g) margarine
salt

For the mini-pizzas:
½ red bell pepper
½ yellow bell pepper
½ green bell pepper
2 champignon mushrooms
3 Tbsp extra-virgin olive oil
thyme
salt and pepper

Preparation time: 20 minutes
Cooking time: 20 minutes
Difficulty: Easy
Calories: 304
Wine: Prosecco di Valdobbiadene

Prepare the puff pastry dough as indicated on p. 10-11. Wash the bell peppers, cut them in half, and eliminate the seeds and the white portions. Cut the peppers into strips (Picture 1) and then into very small cubes. Peel the mushrooms with a sharp knife, removing the stem end where there may be sand or earth. Slice the mushrooms thinly (Picture 2).

1. Heat the extra-virgin olive oil in a pan and toss the bell peppers for a few minutes. Add the mushrooms (Picture 3) and continue cooking. Adjust for salt and pepper.

2. Roll out the pastry dough and cut out small circles with a cookie cutter or similar tool. Spoon the prepared pepper and mushroom mixture into the center of each circle (Picture 4). Season with thyme leaves and bake at 400°F (200°C) for approximately fifteen minutes.

3. Serve the mini-pizzas hot as an appetizer course.

Kitchen tip: To give this dish a different flavor, use zucchini cut into very thin rounds instead of bell peppers. Dust the mini-pizzas with grated parmesan before baking to create a thin crust. Allow to cool slightly before serving.

Millet with Arugula
and Saffron

Serves 4

For the millet:

1 cup (200 g) millet

1 envelope saffron

3 egg yolks

1 bunch arugula

1 ¼ cups (300 g) goat-milk ricotta

2 Tbsp extra-virgin olive oil

2 Tbsp soy sauce

2 shallots

salt

Wash the millet carefully and place it into a sauce pan with three parts salted water and the saffron. Calculate fifteen minutes of cooking time from the moment boiling begins. Remove from heat and allow to cool for approximately five minutes.

1. Slice the shallots and toss them for five minutes in a pan with a small amount of extra-virgin olive oil, the soy sauce, and one tablespoon of water. When the shallots have cooled, add the ricotta and the egg yolks (Picture 1) and cream the ingredients together until they are smooth.

2. Form small, dome-shaped mounds of millet, add the ricotta cream previously prepared, and finish with the fresh arugula. Taste and adjust flavors.

3. Drizzle with extra-virgin olive oil and serve.

Interesting to Know: Millet is an ancient cereal grain that originated in eastern-central Asia. Today, it forms an important part of the diets of African and Asian countries. It is similar to wheat, but it does not contain gluten and is thus ideal for the diets of those with celiac disease. Millet is also the only grain that has an alkalizing effect; as a result, it is indicated for sufferers from acid-stomach.

Preparation time: 15 minutes
Cooking time 20 minutes
Difficulty: Easy
Calories: 366
Wine: Colli di Luni Vermentino

Mozzarella
and Arugula Roll-Ups

Serves 4

For the filling:
½ lb (200 g) mozzarella cheese
2 zucchini, large
1 red bell pepper
1 yellow bell pepper
1 bunch arugula
2 Tbsp extra-virgin olive oil
salt and pepper

Roast the bell peppers over a flame (Picture 1) or else under the broiler until the skin begins to change color. Place in a closed bag to sweat for fifteen minutes.

1. Wash and remove the ends from the zucchini and cut them into thin strips lengthwise. Grill the zucchini for one minute per side. Peel the bell peppers and cut into strips.

2. Wash the arugula and chop. Dress with extra-virgin olive oil and adjust for salt and pepper.

3. Cube the mozzarella and wrap it in two strips of pepper (red and yellow). Close with a slice of grilled zucchini and serve on the seasoned arugula.

Preparation time: 25 minutes
Cooking time: 20 minutes
Difficulty: Easy
Calories: 193
Wine: Bianco di Matelica

Farro Wheat Cassolette
with Rosemary and Pine Nuts

Serves 4

For the cassolette :

2 ¼ cups (250 g) farro
4 Tbsp parmesan cheese
5 Tbsp extra-virgin olive oil
¼ cup (30 g) pine nuts
1 ¼ cups (300 ml) milk
2 cups (500 ml) vegetable broth
2 carrots
1 onion
1 sprig rosemary
1 Tbsp bread crumbs
salt and pepper

Preparation time: 20 minutes
Cooking time: 40 minutes
Difficulty: Easy
Calories: 390
Wine: Piave Pinot Bianco

Clean the carrots and the onion and mince. Sauté with three tablespoons of extra-virgin olive oil and fresh rosemary leaves (Picture 1).

1. Add the broken farro to the sauté (Picture 2), and let it take on flavor in the oil for a few minutes. Add salt and cover with the milk (Picture 3) and half of the hot broth.

2. Cook for twenty minutes. If necessary, add more broth. When it has finished cooking, the farro should be very soft. Add the grated parmesan and adjust for salt and pepper.

3. Brush a cake pan with oil and sprinkle with bread crumbs. Pour in the farro mixture (Picture 4), moisten with a drizzle of olive oil, and sprinkle with pine nuts. Bake at 350°F (180°C) for fifteen to twenty minutes. Serve the cassolette with a seasoned salad of your favorite fresh greens.

Kitchen tip: For an extra touch, dip rosemary sprigs in egg white, roll them in a mixture of poppy and sesame seeds, and fry them in hot oil for a few seconds.

Quinoa Fritters
with Olives and Fennel

Serves 4-6

For the fritters:

1 ⅓ cups (200 g) quinoa

1 fennel bulb

¾ cup (100 g) green olives, pitted

1 egg

¼ cup (30 g) all-purpose flour

6 Tbsp extra-virgin olive oil

parsley and dill

salt and pepper

Wash the fennel bulb. Cut it first into slices (Picture 1) and then into small cubes. Rinse the quinoa in a fine sieve and place it into a sauce pan with twice as much water as quinoa. Add the cubes of fennel. Add salt and cook for twenty to twenty-five minutes.

1. When cooking is complete, remove from heat and set aside to cool. Chop the olives coarsely, wash and chop the herbs, and mix them all with the quinoa.

2. Add the egg and the flour and adjust for salt and pepper. Heat the oil in a non-stick pan and pour it, a spoonful at a time, over the quinoa mixture.

3. Cook the fritters on both sides until they are golden-brown. Dry on a paper towel and serve hot.

Interesting to Know: Quinoa, which looks like tiny seeds similar to lentils, is native to the Andes and was already in cultivation 5000 years ago. Quinoa is suggested for vegetarian diets because it is rich in protein and amino acids. Quinoa also contains Vitamins B1 and B2 (important for the nervous system), niacin (helpful in the metabolism of sugars), and Vitamin C, as well as fiber and minerals such as iron, calcium, and phosphorus.

Preparation time: 25 minutes
Cooking time: 40 minutes
Difficulty: Easy
Calories: 270
Wine: Erbaluce di Caluso

Parmesan Cheese and Black Truffle Soufflé
with Taleggio Sauce

Serves 4

For the soufflé:

2 cups (500 ml) milk

⅓ cup (50 g) all-purpose flour

3 pats butter

1 black truffle

4 eggs

1 cup (100 g) parmesan cheese

salt and pepper

For the sauce:

¾ cup (200 ml) cream, fresh

2 slices taleggio cheese

1 pat butter

2 Tbsp parmesan cheese

salt and pepper

Preparation time: 50 minutes
Cooking time: 30 minutes
Difficulty: Medium
Calories: 459
Wine: Metodo Classico
Franciacorta Rosé

Melt the butter and the flour in a sauce pan (Picture 1) to create a roux. Cook for five minutes.

1. Boil the milk and add it to the roux (which you have allowed to cool in the meantime). Next, add three whole eggs and one egg yolk, the white of one egg beaten until it peaks, and a small amount of grated truffle, the parmesan, salt, and pepper.

2. Butter and lightly flour a series of molds or small soufflé pans (Picture 2). Fill them with the egg and parmesan mixture and bake at 400°F (200°C) for approximately twenty to twenty-five minutes.

3. Prepare the velouté sauce: Boil the cream with the taleggio (Picture 3). When the cheese has melted, adjust for salt and pepper. Finally, add the butter. The sauce should remain glossy.

4. Distribute the taleggio sauce on the plate, overturn the soufflé, and grate the remaining truffle on the plate. Finish with a dusting of parmesan.

Interesting to Know: Roux, made with butter and flour, is generally used to bind or emulsify sauces.

Herbed Eggplant and Caprino Cheese
with Apple Cider Vinegar Dressing

Serves 4

For the eggplant:

2 eggplant, long variety, small
2 pieces caprino cheese, aged
4 cups (1 lt) sunflower or other light vegetable oil for frying
salt and pepper

For the dressing:

6 tbsp apple cider vinegar
1 tsp acacia honey
a pinch hot pepper
2 Tbsp all-purpose flour
1 sprig marjoram
3 Tbsp extra-virgin olive oil
salt

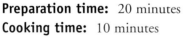

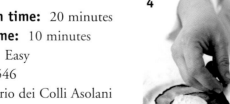

Wash the eggplant carefully, dry, and cut into rounds approximately ¼ inch (½ cm) thick (Picture 1). In a deep pan or pot, heat the oil to proper frying temperature.

1. Flour the eggplant lightly, fry in the hot oil until it is a golden color, and drain on a paper towel. Lay the slices of eggplant in a bowl (Picture 2) and season with salt.

2. Heat the vinegar in a small sauce pan for a few minutes with the hot pepper. Remove from heat, add the honey and one-half teaspoon salt, and allow to cool. Add the oil to the vinegar and pour both over the eggplant (Picture 3). Allow the flavors to blend for approximately ten minutes.

3. Cut the caprino cheeses into rounds about ½ inch (1 cm) thick and arrange them over the eggplant (Picture 4). Dust with pepper and garnish with the marjoram.

Interesting to Know: Marination is a method that is appropriate for both meat and vegetables, but is especially well suited to fish. Whatever food is marinated, the objective is always the same: enhance flavor, tenderize, and improve preservation.

Preparation time: 20 minutes
Cooking time: 10 minutes
Difficulty: Easy
Calories: 546
Wine: Falerio dei Colli Asolani

Robiola Cheese with Spiced Honey
and Pistachios

Serves 4

For the cheese:

1 ⅓ cups (350 g) robiola cheese
⅔ cup (150 ml) cream, fresh
1 gelatin leaf
2 Tbsp milk
⅓ cup (40 g) confectioner's sugar
⅓ cup (40 g) pistachios
5 Tbsp (100 g) acacia honey
2 Tbsp (20 g) raisins
1 tsp mixed spices, powdered
(cardamom seeds, cinnamon,
cloves, cumin, pepper)

Preparation time: 15 minutes
Cooking time: 1 hour
Difficulty: Easy
Calories: 410
Wine: Muffato della Sala

Soak the raisins in warm water. Separately, soak the gelatin in cold water. Stir the robiola cheese in a bowl until it is soft.

1. Blanch the pistachios for one minute in boiling water, drain, eliminate the membrane that covers the nuts, and roast them in the oven or in a sauté pan long enough to dry them. Crush them coarsely in a mortar or mince them with a knife and add to the robiola.

2. Over low heat, dissolve the gelatin in two tablespoons of milk, let cool, and add to the cheese.

3. Whisk the cream with a French whip, add the confectioner's sugar, and blend with the cheese, mixing gently. Cover and store in the refrigerator.

4. Heat the honey with the spices, one tablespoon of water, and the raisins squeezed to remove excess liquid. Using a pair of spoons, form "quenelles" or dollops of cheese and pistachios, moisten with the spiced honey, and serve.

A suggestion for preparing the cheese "quenelles." Wet a pair of spoons in hot water (Picture 1). Using one of them, remove a spoonful of the mixture and then pass it back and forth between the bowls of the two spoons to smooth and shape the cheese (Pictures 2-3-4).

Vegetable Croquettes
with Parmesan Cheese

Serves 4

For the croquettes:
¾ lb (400 g) potatoes
⅓ lb (200 g) carrots
1 clove garlic
1 small bunch parsley
2 cups (200 g) parmesan cheese
2-3 eggs
Bread crumbs
Salt and pepper

For the sauce:
1 container low-fat yogurt
2 Tbsp mayonnaise

Preparation time: 15 minutes
Cooking time: 50 minutes
Difficulty: Easy
Calories: 402
Wine: Valcalepio Bianco

Peel and wash the potatoes and the carrots. Cut them into pieces and boil in salted water in two separate pots for approximately twenty minutes.

1. In the meantime, finely mince the garlic and the parsley together. Drain the potatoes and the carrots. When they are ready, mash with a ricer or potato masher.

2. Pour the potato and carrot mixture into an ample container. Add the minced garlic and parsley (Picture 1), the eggs, the parmesan, and bread crumbs (Picture 2) sufficient to create a compact mixture. Mix well to blend. Season with salt and pepper.

3. Shape small croquettes with an ice cream scoop (Picture 3). Line a baking sheet with parchment or non-stick oven paper, arrange the croquettes on the paper, and bake them at 350°F (180°C) for approximately thirty minutes.

4. Prepare the sauce: Mix the yogurt together with the mayonnaise. Serve the croquettes hot, accompanied by the freshly made sauce and a mixed salad.

Balsamic-Infused Mesclun
in Bread Bowls

Serves 4

For the bread bowls
2 pieces Sardinian carasau bread

For the salad:
2 bunches mesclun
¼ lb (120 g) gorgonzola, sweet
3 Tbsp walnuts
3 Tbsp pine nuts
¼ cup (40 g) raisins

For the dressing:
8 Tbsp extra-virgin olive oil
8 Tbsp balsamic vinegar
salt and pepper

Soften the carasau bread in a bowl or basin with cold water and divide into two parts.

1. Turn four cups upside down on a baking sheet and wrap the softened bread around them. Place in the oven for approximately fifteen minutes to dry. Allow them to cool and unmold.

2. In the meantime, wash the salad greens and tear into pieces with your hands. Cut the cheese into small cubes and break the nuts into small chunks.

3. Mix together the salad ingredients and serve in the bread bowls. Dress with a pinch of salt, pepper, oil (a newly pressed extra-virgin oil would be particularly appropriate for this recipe), and balsamic vinegar.

Kitchen tip: This recipe lends itself to numerous variations. In the place of mesclun, use other salad greens with a slightly bitter or peppery taste such as green radicchietto (a variety of chicory local to the Trieste area). If gorgonzola is not to your taste, use non-blue cheeses without veining—as long as they have a flavor that is sufficiently intense to provide a contrast to the vinegar. Shaved pecorino or parmesan also work well.

Preparation time: 25 minutes
Cooking time: 15 minutes
Difficulty: Easy
Calories: 384
Wine: Roero Arneis

Porcini Mushroom
Mini-Strudel

Serves 6

For the puff pastry:
2 ½ cups (320 g) all-purpose flour
⅔ cup (160 ml) water
1 ⅔ cups (400 g) margarine
salt

For the filling:
1 ¼ lb (600 g) porcini mushrooms
5 Tbsp extra-virgin olive oil
1 egg yolk
2 Tbsp parsley
1 hot pepper
2 cloves garlic
salt

Prepare the puff pastry dough according to the directions given on p. 10-11. Clean the porcini mushrooms well, removing the end of the stem. Cut them into thin slices. Chop the parsley and the hot pepper and set aside.

1. Peel and slightly smash the cloves of garlic and sauté in a pan with olive oil. When the garlic is well browned, remove and discard.

2. Add the porcini mushrooms (Picture 1), allow the vegetable liquid to evaporate, and add the salt, the parsley, and the hot pepper. Cook for approximately one minute. Remove from heat and allow to cool.

3. Roll out the pastry dough and cut it into squares approximately 4 inches (10 cm) on a side. On each, place a tablespoon of mushrooms drained of their cooking liquid (Picture 2). Cover with a second square of dough (Picture 3), dampen your fingers with cold water, and press firmly on the edges to ensure that the "packet" remains sealed.

4. Decorate the surface with the leftover pastry dough. Brush the strudels with beaten egg yolk and bake at 350°F (180°C) for approximately ten minutes.

5. When the strudels have puffed up slightly and the surface is a uniform golden-brown, remove from the oven, arrange them on plates, and serve hot.

Preparation time: 15 minutes
Cooking time: 20 minutes
Difficulty: Easy
Calories: 601
Wine: Trentino Pinot Nero

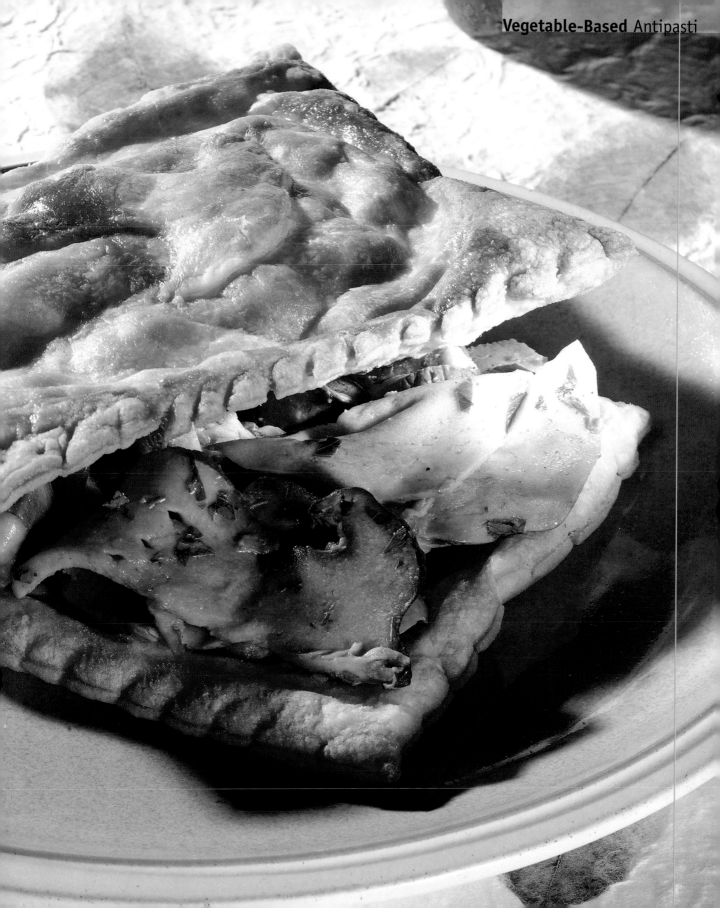

Tomato Terrine
with Basil Pesto

Serves 4

For the terrine:
1 ¾ lb (800 g) red tomatoes
½ lb (200 g) mozzarella
½ cup (60 g) taggiasca olives, black
1 leaf gelatin
2 Tbsp parsley, basil and oregano
⅓ cup (100 ml) vegetable broth

For the basil pesto:
⅔ cup (30 g) basil
3 Tbsp extra-virgin olive oil
2 Tbsp lemon juice
salt and pepper

Preparation time: 40 minutes
Cooking time: 30 minutes
Difficulty: Medium
Calories: 312
Wine: Regaleali Bianco

Soak the gelatin in cold water (Picture 1). Blanch the tomatoes in boiling water for thirty seconds, peel and remove seeds, and cut into cubes. Place the tomatoes in a colander to drain any remaining liquid.

1. Cut the mozzarella into thin strips (Picture 2) and lay the strips on an absorbent paper towel to dry.

2. Heat the broth. In it, dissolve the gelatin, drained and squeezed, and allow to cool, being careful that it does not solidify. Add the chopped herbs, the tomato cubes, and the taggiasca olives. Adjust for salt and pepper.

3. Pour the mixture into a terrine mold lined with plastic wrap. Insert the strips of mozzarella (Picture 3) and place in the refrigerator to harden for at least two hours.

4. In the meantime, combine the basil, oil, lemon, salt, and pepper (Picture 4) and whip them together in a food processor or mixer to create a pesto.

5. Serve the tomato terrine sliced, accompanied by a fresh salad of seasonal greens and seasoned with the basil pesto.

Tomato and Eggplant Puffs

Serves 4

For the puffs:
¾ cup (100 g) all-purpose flour
3 Tbsp (50 ml) water
½ cup (125 g) margarine
1 egg
salt

For the filling:
¾ lb (300 g) eggplant
½ lb (250 g) tomatoes
¼ lb (120 g) mozzarella
5-6 basil leaves
1 clove garlic
3 Tbsp extra-virgin olive oil
salt and pepper

Preparation time: 20 minutes
Cooking time: 30 minutes
Difficulty: Easy
Calories: 390
Wine: Greco di Tufo

Prepare the puff pastry dough according to the directions found on p. 10-11. Extend the dough on a floured surface and shape triangles approximately 2-½ to 3-½ inches (7-8 cm) on each side.

1. Arrange the triangles on a baking sheet, brush them with the beaten egg, and sprinkle with a pinch of salt. Bake at 350°F (180°C) for fifteen to twenty minutes.

2. Peel the eggplant, cut into cubes, and boil for two to three minutes. Drain the eggplant and set aside to cool.

3. Scald the tomatoes in boiling water and peel (Picture 1). Remove the seeds and cut the pulp into cubes (Picture 2). Cube the mozzarella as well.

4. Brown the clove of garlic with the oil in a sauté pan. Add the eggplant, the basil leaves, and the tomato. Season with salt and pepper and cook for two to three minutes. Incorporate the mozzarella and mix.

5. Cut the already-cooked pastry puffs in half and fill with eggplant, tomatoes, and mozzarella. Close the puffs and serve immediately.

1

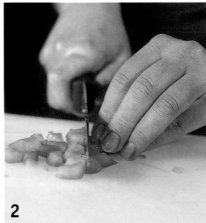
2

Individual Quiches
with Swiss Chard and Artichokes

Serves 6-8

For the pastry dough:
2 ½ cups (300 g) all-purpose flour
1 stick (120 g) butter
salt

For the vegetable filling:
⅔ lb (300 g) Swiss chard
⅓ cup (100 ml) cream, fresh
3 Tbsp parmesan cheese
1 pat butter
2 artichokes
2 green onions
2 eggs
2 Tbsp extra-virgin olive oil
salt and pepper

Preparation time: 30 minutes
Cooking time: 50 minutes
Difficulty: Easy
Calories: 407
Wine: Colli di Conegliano Bianco

Knead the ingredients for the dough together for some time, making sure to use cold water (for the procedure, see p. 12 of the Introduction).

1. Wash the green onions (Picture 1), cut them into thin rounds, and sauté gently in butter in a non-stick pan. Wash and drain the Swiss chard and cut into thin strips (Picture 2). Place the chard into the pan with the green onions, season with salt, and add a small amount of water. Mix and cook, covered, for approximately five minutes.

2. Clean the artichokes, eliminating the tough outer leaves, the spines, and the fuzz or choke above the heart. Slice thinly and toss in a pan with two tablespoons of olive oil for two to three minutes.

3. Pour all of the vegetables into a bowl and add the eggs, the cream, the grated parmesan, salt, and pepper. Stir carefully, making sure to blend well.

4. Lightly butter a series of small aluminium molds and line them with the pastry dough (Picture 3). Remove the extra dough from the edges with a knife and fill the molds with the vegetable mixture (Picture 4). Cook the quiches in a 350°F (180°C) oven for thirty-five minutes. Unmo and serve warm, garnishing with shavings of your favorite cheese.

Mini-Pizzas
with Radicchio and Melted Taleggio

Serves 4

For the dough:
2 ½ cups (300 g) all-purpose flour
½ packet brewer's yeast
2 Tbsp extra-virgin olive oil
½ cup (130 ml) water
salt

For the topping:
3 Tbsp extra-virgin olive oil
⅓ lb (200 g) red radicchio
⅕ lb (100 g) taleggio cheese
chives
salt and pepper

Pour the warm water into a cup, add the oil and the yeast and, mixing with a fork, dissolve the yeast. Pour the flour into a bowl and add the yeast and oil mixture. Add a pinch of salt and knead energetically until the resulting dough is smooth and thoroughly blended. Form the dough into a ball, cover the bowl with plastic wrap, and set aside to rise for forty-five minutes in a warm place.

1. Remove the leaves from the heads of radicchio, wash them, dry them with a dish towel, and cut them into thin strips. Heat the oil in a pan. When the oil is hot, add the radicchio. Season lightly with salt and pepper and sauté for no more than two minutes. The radicchio should remain flavorful and "al dente."

2. Roll out the pizza dough to a thickness of approximately 1/4 inch (1/2 cm). Using a biscuit cutter or the rim of a glass, cut out circles approximately 3-4 inches (8-10 cm) in diameter.

3. Distribute a tablespoon of the radicchio mixture on the dough circle and add a few strips of taleggio cheese (Picture 1). Arrange the mini-pizzas on a lightly buttered and floured baking sheet and cook for twenty minutes at 350°F (180°C). When they are done, sprinkle with minced chives and serve immediately.

Preparation time: 25 minutes
Cooking time: 45 minutes
Difficulty: Medium
Calories: 459
Wine: Etna Rosato

1

Soy Bread Terrine
with Spring Vegetables

Serves 4

For the terrine:

1 soy bread, French loaf

3 carrots

3 champignon mushrooms

2 zucchini

1 head red radicchio

3 Tbsp extra-virgin olive oil

chives

salt and white pepper

Wash the zucchini and remove the ends, peel the carrots and the mushrooms, and eliminate the stalk end of the radicchio.

1. Cut the carrots and the zucchini into strips (Picture 1). Slice the mushrooms thinly. Remove the radicchio leaves from the head and eliminate the white "rib" in the middle of each leaf. Boil the zucchini and the carrots in salted water for two minutes.

2. Cut the bread lengthwise into five slices of the same thickness and then reform the loaf, alternating the vegetables with salt, pepper, and oil.

3. Compress the loaf and wrap tightly in aluminium foil that has been oiled and sprinkled with whole chives. Bake at 375°F (190°C) for twelve minutes and serve hot.

Kitchen tip: During the winter, substitute squash, sliced and baked, for the zucchini. If you use squash, moisten the bread with a small amount of milk so that the cooking time can be extended by five minutes without drying out the terrine.

Preparation time: 10 minutes
Cooking time: 10 minutes
Difficulty: Easy
Calories: 149
Wine: Pinot Bianco

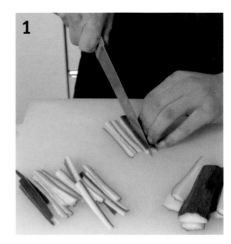

Oregano Pastry Cups
with Cherry Tomatoes and Mozzarella

Serves 4

For the puff pastry:
½ cup (60 g) all-purpose flour
3 Tbsp (30 ml) water
⅓ cup (75 g) margarine
salt

For the vegetables:
½ lb (200 g) cherry tomatoes
4 Tbsp parmesan cheese
2 mozzarella
1 tsp Oregano, leaf
2 cloves garlic
2 Tbsp extra-virgin olive oil
salt and pepper

Prepare the puff pastry according to the instructions on p. 10-11. Allow the pastry dough to soften and roll it into a thin layer. Line single-serving baking tins or ramekins with the dough (Picture 1).

1. Wash the tomatoes, remove seeds, and cut them in half. Cut the mozzarella into thin slices and dry on absorbent paper towelling. Distribute the tomatoes over the pastry dough, alternating with slices of mozzarella.

2. Sprinkle with thin slices of garlic, grated parmesan (Picture 2), oregano, salt, and pepper, and drizzle with extra-virgin olive oil. Bake at 350°F (180°C) for twenty-five minutes.

3. Remove the pastry cups from the oven and allow to cool. Serve with a salad of frisée or curly endive dressed with a drizzle of extra-virgin olive oil and a little salt.

Kitchen tip: To speed up preparation time, use pre-packaged puff pastry dough.

Preparation time: 10 minutes
Cooking time: 20 minutes
Difficulty: Easy
Calories: 200
Wine: Malvasia Istriana

Beignets
with Leeks and Fondue

Serves 6

For the beignet dough:
¾ stick (80 g) butter
1 ¼ cups (150 g) all-purpose flour
4 eggs
1 tsp parsley
10 Tbsp parmesan cheese
1 cup (250 ml) water
salt

For the filling:
2 pats butter
¼ cup (25 g) all-purpose flour
¾ cup (200 ml) milk
½ small leek
7 Tbsp parmesan cheese
1 egg
nutmeg
salt and pepper

For the fondue:
2 pats butter
1 cup (250 ml) milk
⅓ cup (100 ml) cream, fresh
1 Tbsp (10 g) all-purpose flour
7 Tbsp parmesan cheese
1 egg yolk
salt

Preparation time: 40 minutes
Cooking time: 15 minutes
Difficulty: Medium
Calories: 628
Wine: Erbaluce di Caluso

Place the water, the butter cut into pats, and a small amount of salt into a sauce pan. Bring to a boil, add the flour, and cook stirring, for two minutes.

1. Set aside to cool. Add the eggs, the grated parmesan, and the chopped parsley. Blend to obtain a thick and sticky mixture. Heat the oven to 350°F (180°C). Place the beignet dough in a pastry sack and create small mounds on a buttered and floured baking sheet (Picture 1). Cook the beignets for twenty-five minutes, Remove from the oven and allow to cool.

2. Clean the leek, cut it into rounds, and brown it in approximately 1 pat of butter for three minutes.

3. Dissolve the butter in a sauce pan. Add the flour and fry for one minute. Add the milk and the cream and simmer for two minutes. Remove from heat and add the grated parmesan and the egg yolk. Whip and season with salt.

4. Cut the beignets in half and fill each with the leek mixture (Pictures 2-3). Heat them for two to three minutes at 350°F (180°C). Dust the serving dishes with grated parmesan, distribute two tablespoons of the fondue, and arrange the beignets on the plates. Serve immediately.

2

3

1

Diamond-Shaped Mini-Pizzas
with Squash and Dried Fruit

Serves 4

For the dough:
1 cup (150 g) semolina
¾ cup (100 g) all-purpose flour
½ packet brewer's yeast
⅔ cup (150 ml) water
1 Tbsp extra-virgin olive oil

For the squash:
⅔ lb (300 g) squash (flesh only)
2 pats butter
3 sage leaves
3 Tbsp (50 g) apricots, dried
2 Tbsp (20 g) raisins
2 small slices Brie
2 Tbsp extra-virgin olive oil
salt

Dissolve the brewer's yeast in warm water in a large bowl. Add the semolina, the all-purpose flour, and the olive oil. Knead until the dough is smooth and soft.

1. Cover the bowl with the dough with plastic wrap and set aside in a warm place to rise for forty-five minutes.

2. Cut the squash into cubes. Dissolve the butter in a pan. As soon as it begins to boil, add the cubed squash. Season lightly with salt and cook for five to seven minutes.

3. Cut the raisins and the apricots into small pieces and slice the sage leaves thinly. Roll the dough out on your work surface to a thickness of approximately ¼ inch (½ cm). Using a knife or a smooth-bladed cutter, cut out diamond shapes approximately 2 inches (5 cm) on each side (Picture 1).

4. Distribute the diamonds of dough on a lightly oiled baking sheet (Picture 2). Spoon the squash onto them (Picture 3), and sprinkle with the apricots, raisins, and strips of sage. Arrange a thin slice of Brie on each diamond. Bake at 350°F (180°C) for ten to thirteen minutes. Remove from the oven and serve hot.

Preparation time: 30 minutes
Cooking time: 20 minutes
Difficulty: Easy
Calories: 437
Wine: Ribolla Gialla

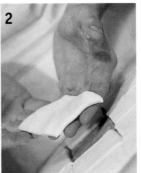

Porcini Mille Feuille
with Frico Crackers

Serves 4

For the porcini:
8 large porcini mushrooms
4 Tbsp extra-virgin olive oil
1 clove garlic
1 bay leaf
salt

For the frico crackers:
⅓ lb (190 g) montasio cheese
1 pat butter
1 sprig rosemary
2 leaves sage
salt

For the bread:
4 slices sandwich bread
4 Tbsp extra-virgin olive oil
⅓ cup (30 g) parmesan cheese

Preparation time: 40 minutes
Cooking time: 15 minutes
Difficulty: Medium
Calories: 527
Wine: Refosco dal Peduncolo Rosso

Clean the porcini, being sure to eliminate any remaining dirt or sand. Remove the stems and wash the mushrooms. Cube four stems and set aside.

1. Brown the clove of garlic and the bay leaf in olive oil. Next, brown the whole porcini caps for approximately two minutes per side. Add salt and remove the mushrooms from the pan.

2. Mince the sage with the rosemary and brown it in butter in the same pan used for the porcini caps. Add the cubed mushrooms stems (Picture 1) and adjust for salt.

3. After three to four minutes, add the Montasio cheese in cubes (Picture 2). Melt the cheese until it blends with the mushrooms (Picture 3). Pour the hot cheese and mushroom mixture onto a plate, spreading to a thickness of about ½ inch (1 cm). When the mixture begins to cool, cut out circle-shaped crackers approximately 3-4 inches (8-10 cm) in diameter.

4. Heat the olive oil in another pan, cut the bread slices into circles about 4-¾ inches (12 cm) in diameter and fry them for two to three minutes until they are golden-brown.

5. Arrange the bread circles on serving plates. Cover each circle with a porcini cap, a frico cracker, and another porcini cap. Sprinkle with a few shavings of parmesan and serve immediately.

Tasty Bread Bites
with Three Unique Toppings

Serves 4

For the bread:
½ lb (250 g) French bread

For the first topping:
¼ lb (150 g) zucchini
8 thin slices bacon
1 sprig chives
3 Tbsp parmesan cheese
2 Tbsp extra-virgin olive oil
salt and pepper

For the second topping:
1 cup (150 g) fava beans, shelled
¼ lb (150 g) bell peppers, red and yellow
1 slice fontina
3 Tbsp extra-virgin olive oil
salt and pepper

For the third topping:
1 small leek
½ cup (40 g) walnuts
1 small slice gorgonzola, sweet
1 Tbsp chopped parsley
2 Tbsp extra-virgin olive oil
salt and pepper

Preparation time: 25 minutes
Cooking time: 5 minutes
Difficulty: Easy
Calories: 327
Wine: Prosecco di Conegliano Brut

Cut the bread into diagonal slices approximately ½ inch (1 cm) thick and arrange them on a baking sheet.

1. Prepare the first topping: Clean the zucchini and cut them into sticks about 1 to 2 inches (4-5 cm) in length. Cut the bacon into strips and brown in olive oil, together with the zucchini, for two to three minutes (Picture 1). Remove from heat and set aside.

2. Prepare the second topping: Boil the fava beans for two to three minutes in salted water. Drain, set aside to cool, and shell. Cube the bell peppers and sauté in olive oil in the same pan in which the zucchini were cooked. Add the fava beans, adjust flavors, season with salt, and set aside.

3. Prepare the final topping: Cut the leek into rounds and brown in oil for two to three minutes in the pan used previously. Add the coarsely chopped walnuts and season with salt, pepper, and the chopped parsley.

4. Arrange the toppings on the bread slices (Picture 2). Sprinkle the first with minced chives and parmesan, the second with fontina, and the last with the gorgonzola (Picture 3).

5. Heat the oven to 375°F (190°C). Crust the bread bites for five minutes. Remove from the oven and serve immediately.

Fish-Based Antipasti

Sole Pinwheels
with Arugula and Quail Egg Salad

Serves 4

For the pinwheels:
4 sole fillets ¼ lb (250 g) each
¼ lb (100 g) salmon, fresh
1 cup (100 g) spinach, raw

For the salad:
2 bunches arugula
1 cucumber
4 red tomatoes

For the eggs:
8 quail eggs

For the anchovy sauce:
4 anchovies, salt-preserved
⅔ lb (300 g) Tuscan bread
6 Tbsp extra-virgin olive oil
2 Tbsp red wine vinegar
salt and pepper

Skin the sole and separate the four fillets. Flatten each with a meat tenderizer. Slice the salmon and arrange the slices over the sole fillets (Picture 1).

1. Wash the spinach leaves and remove the stems. Place the spinach leaves over the sole (Picture 2). Role the sole and let stand in the refrigerator for a few minutes.

2. Carefully wash the arugula several times and cook it in boiling water for one minute. Drain and chill in cold water.

3. Place the quail eggs in a pot with water and boil them for one minute. Cool them immediately under running water and peel, being careful not to break the eggs. Peel the cucumber and cut it into small cubes. Peel the tomatoes then seed and hollow them and cut the flesh into cubes.

4. Slice the bread about ¼ inch (½ cm) thick and cut the slices into cubes. Distribute the cubes on a baking sheet with oil, salt, pepper, and the chopped anchovies. Add a small amount of vinegar, oil, and pepper and marinate for a few minutes.

5. Dress the sole pinwheels with oil, salt, and pepper, and steam for three minutes. Stem the arugula as well to heat. Plate the arugula and arrange the pinwheels on top (Picture 3). Sprinkle with the sauce and drizzle with extra-virgin olive oil.

Preparation time: 40 minutes
Cooking time: 15 minutes
Difficulty: Medium
Calories: 383
Wine: Friuli Isonzo Sauvignon

Sautéed Squid
over Croutons

Serves 4

For the sauté:

8 small-medium squid

2 San Marzano tomatoes

2 cloves garlic

2 Tbsp extra-virgin olive oil

1 hot red pepper

¼ cup white wine

2 slices country-style Italian bread

1 sprig rosemary

parsley

salt and pepper

Wash the squid, carefully removing the internal organs and skin (Picture 1). Cut the squid into rings. Seed the tomatoes and dice them coarsely (Picture 2).

1. Peel and smash the garlic and place it in a pan with the oil and the chopped hot pepper. Sauté gently and then add the squid (Picture 3), tossing for about two minutes. Add the white wine and allow the liquid to evaporate. Add the chopped parsley, the rosemary, and the tomato. Season with salt and pepper and cook, semi-covered, for five minutes.

2. While the squid is cooking, cut the bread into croutons and toast it under the broiler. Divide the croutons among four bowls.

3. Serve the squid in the bowls, moistening the croutons with the pot liquor.

Interesting to Know: Like many cooking and gastronomic terms, "sauté" comes from French and means to "brown quickly" or "cook over a high flame." By extension, sauté also refers to dishes cooked using this method.

Preparation time: 15 minutes
Cooking time: 10 minutes
Difficulty: Easy
Calories: 219
Wine: Vermentino di Sardegna

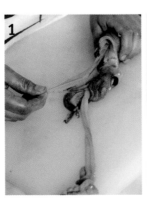

Octopus Puff Pastry
with Potatoes and Black Olives

Serves 4

For the pastry:

20 small vol-au-vent shells

⅔ lb (300 g) octopus

¼ lb (100 g) celery root

¼ lb (100 g) fennel root

½ cup (50 g) black olives, pitted

4 Tbsp extra-virgin olive oil

2 potatoes

1 bay leaf

2 Tbsp capers

¼ cup white wine

1 small bunch parsley

salt and pepper

Preparation time: 20 minutes
Cooking time: 30 minutes
Difficulty: Easy
Calories: 295
Wine: Pinot Bianco del Piave

Cook the octopus in a large pot for thirty minutes together with the bay leaf, the white wine, the celery root, the fennel bulb, and the whole potatoes (Picture 1).

1. Chop the parsley and mix with the black olives broken into pieces and the capers coarsely chopped with a knife.

2. Cut the octopus into small pieces. Peel the potatoes and cut them into small cubes. Mix all the ingredients together, season with salt and pepper, and dress with extra-virgin olive oil.

3. Heat or cook the pastry in the oven, allow to cool, and fill with the octopus mixture. Garnish with a few dill leaves and serve immediately.

Interesting to Know: Octopus may be prepared in an enormous variety of ways. After first cooking as indicated in this recipe, try baking the sliced octopus in a 475°F (250°C) oven for five minutes together with a clove of garlic, a drizzle of olive oil, and some thyme. Plate and serve with ¼ lb (100 g) of fennel bulb and ¾ lb (400 g) of puntarella chicory (sliced extremely thinly), cilantro, small slices of candied tomato, or shavings of black truffle. Finish with a citronette dressing made with olive oil, a small amount of lemon juice, and chopped black truffle.

Fig and Smoked Salmon
Tartines

Serves 4

For the tartines:
8 slices baguette
3 figs
¼ lb (80 g) smoked salmon
1 green lemon
chives
white pepper

Wash the figs and cut them into fairly thick slices. Lightly pepper the slices and set aside.

1. Toast the bread slices under the broiler set to its highest setting. Remove from the oven and place a slice of fig on each.

2. Next, add one strip of salmon sliced extremely thinly. Sprinkle with white pepper and garnish with chopped chives and the lemon cut into triangles.

3. Serve the fig and salmon tartines with the appetizer course.

Kitchen tip: Here's a more traditional variation on this recipe. In a small amount of oil, sauté a shallot. Add washed, seeded, and diced peppers and toss. Add two carrots cut into rounds. Cut two zucchini into small cubes, add to the other vegetables, and season with salt and pepper. When cooking is complete, add ten pitted black olives. The result is a vegetable "ragù" that is an excellent alternative to other toppings for canapés and toast.

Preparation time: 15 minutes
Cooking time: 5 minutes
Difficulty: Easy
Calories: 178
Wine: Trentino Müller Thurgau

Scallops Au Gratin
with Porcini Mushrooms

Serves 4

For the scallops:
8 scallops
4 porcini mushrooms
3 Tbsp bread crumbs
1 clove garlic
2 Tbsp extra-virgin olive oil
parsley
salt and pepper

Wash the scallops carefully under cold running water.

1. Clean the porcini gently and carefully with a damp paper towel and eliminate the root end with its sand or dirt. Once the mushrooms are clean, cut them into small pieces (Pictures 1-2).

2. Smash the garlic clove and cut it in half. Heat a non-stick pan with the extra-virgin olive oil and sauté the garlic until it is golden. Blanch the scallops (Picture 3), add the mushrooms, and toss briefly. Season with salt and pepper and dust with the chopped parsley.

3. Cover the scallops with the mushrooms, sprinkle with bread crumbs, and drizzle lightly with cold-pressed olive oil. Place them under the broiler to crust.

Interesting to Know: Au gratin cooking or "crusting" is employed toward the end of the preparation of a dish. Because crusting is a difficult process that requires exact timing, it is not generally used as an overall cooking method. Rather, a dish is first prepared in the oven or in a pan (as in this recipe) and then passed under a salamander grill or broiler, which forms the classic golden-brown crust on its surface.

Preparation time: 10 minutes
Cooking time: 15 minutes
Difficulty: Easy
Calories: 101
Wine: Lugana

Spicy Seafood Sauté

Serves 4

For the seafood sauté:

½ lb (250 g) smooth Venus clams
½ lb (200 g) mussels
½ lb (250 g) clams
5 cherry tomatoes
2 cloves garlic
3 Tbsp extra-virgin olive oil
¼ cup white wine
1 hot red pepper
4 slices home-made bread
Parsley
Salt

Wash the clams and mussels carefully, repeating several times. Scrub the clams and eliminate the brown threads attached to the mussels. Allow them all to purge, each in a separate salt-water bath.

1. Wash and cut the tomatoes into four parts and chop the parsley. In a sauce pan, heat the extra-virgin olive oil and add one clove of minced garlic, the crumbled hot pepper, and a small amount of parsley.

2. Add the smooth Venus clams, increase the heat, and cook for three minutes. Flavor with the wine and add the mussels and other clams. Allow to come to a boil once again, add the tomatoes (Picture 1) and the remaining parsley, and cook, covered, until the clams and mussels open.

3. Toast the bread, rub lightly with garlic (Picture 2), and place onto serving plates as a base for the hot seafood sauté.

Interesting to Know: The process of "purging" clams, mussels, and other bivalves is essential for eliminating the sand that may remain inside the shells and which cannot be removed with simple washing. The series of water "baths," to which a healthy amount of salt is added, allows the shellfish to "breathe" and expel the sand.

Preparation time: 20 minutes
Cooking time: 15 minutes
Difficulty: Easy
Calories: 219
Wine: Ischia Bianco

Potato, Bell Pepper,
and Marinated Mackerel Salad

Serves 4

For the salad:

1 lb (500 g) mackerel, fresh
1 lemon
6 Tbsp extra-virgin olive oil, light
4 potatoes, medium-large
½ red bell pepper
parsley
salt and pepper

Fillet and debone the mackerel. Wash the fillets and place them on a plate. Dress with a vinaigrette of lemon juice, salt, pepper, and a few leaves of chopped parsley (Picture 1). Cover with plastic wrap and marinate in the refrigerator overnight.

1. Place the potatoes in cold, salted water, and bring to a boil, cooking until they are tender at the center. Drain and allow to cool.

2. Wash the peppers and slice into strips. Peel the potatoes. Cut them into slices and then into small cubes (Picture 2). Dress with the bell peppers, salt, pepper, oil, and chopped parsley.

3. Drain the mackerel and cut into bite-sized pieces. Arrange the fish over the vegetables and serve.

Interesting to Know: The custom of eating fish raw comes from the Far East. Marinating raw fish, however, is obviously different from the classic sushi, which requires the fish to be sliced just before it is served.

Preparation time: 15 minutes
Cooking time: 20 minutes
Difficulty: Easy
Calories: 313
Wine: Sicilia Chardonnay

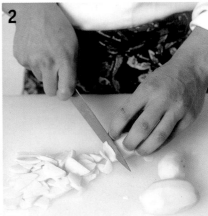

Savoy Cabbage, Tuna,
and Mozzarella Canapés

Serves 4

For the canapés:
½ baguette or thin French loaf
2 fillets oil-packed tuna
2 Tbsp black olives, pitted
⅓ lb (150 g) mozzarella
¼ Savoy cabbage head
1 clove garlic
2 Tbsp olive oil
oregano
salt and pepper

Slice the bread and toast under the broiler. Cut the Savoy cabbage finely and simmer for ten minutes in a pan with the extra-virgin olive oil and the clove of garlic, smashed. Season with salt and pepper (Picture 1).

1. Distribute one teaspoon of Savoy cabbage on each toast round and, above the cabbage, arrange a piece of tuna and one olive.

2. Cut the mozzarella into small discs, making use of a cookie cutter or similar if you like (Picture 2), and place atop the other ingredients (Picture 3).

3. Crust under the broiler for five minutes and sprinkle with oregano. Serve hot.

Kitchen tip: Here's an alternative for canapés. Cube an eggplant and chop one shallot. Sauté the shallot in olive oil over low heat. Add the eggplant and season with salt and pepper. Cook, stirring frequently. Flavor with thyme and set aside to cool. Peel a boiled potato, add to the vegetables, and whip together in a blender or food processor. Toast bread rounds in the oven at 350°F (180°C) for five minutes and serve with the eggplant cream. You can also add, over the eggplant, half of a bell pepper, sliced into very thin strips, dredged in corn meal, and fried in sunflower or other light vegetable oil.

Preparation time: 20 minutes
Cooking time: 15 minutes
Difficulty: Easy
Calories: 377
Wine: Colli di Luni Bianco

134

Salt-Cod
and Potato Tart

Serves 4

For the tart:

1 lb (400 g) salt cod
¾ lb (400 g) potatoes
1 onion
2 cups (500 ml) milk
¾ cup (200 ml) cream
½ cup white wine
1 Tbsp thyme and marjoram
salt and pepper

On the side:

1 cup (150 g) fava beans, shelled
4 tomatoes, vine-fresh
4 Tbsp extra-virgin olive oil
1 clove garlic
marjoram
salt

Preparation time: 20 minutes
Cooking time: 1 hour and
20 minutes
Difficulty: Medium
Calories: 310
Wine: Friuli Isonzo Sauvignon

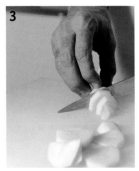

Soak the salt-cod in cold water for two days to remove salt, changing the water several times.

1. Shell the fava beans, parboil, and eliminate the skin. Remove the skin from the salt-cod and cut it into small pieces. Peel the potatoes and cut half of them into cubes.

2. In a pan, brown the onion with the salt-cod and the potatoes (Picture 1). Cook for a few minutes and then add the white wine. Allow the liquid to evaporate. Add the milk (Picture 2) and cook for forty minutes. Halfway through the cooking process, add the cream, adjust for salt and pepper, and sprinkle with the chopped fines herbs.

3. Cut the remaining potatoes into slices (Picture 3) and boil them in salted water. Blanch the tomatoes, cool them in iced water, peel and remove seeds, and slice (Picture 4).

4. Butter a series of molds and layer the potatoes and the salt-cod mixture into them. Crust in the oven and serve with the fresh fava beans and the tomato fillets tossed with olive oil, garlic, and marjoram.

Fresh Tuna Fillet
with Green Onions and Fava Beans

Serves 4

For the tuna:

¾ lb (380 g) tuna fillet, fresh

1 clove garlic

4 Tbsp extra-virgin olive oil

lemon thyme

chives

rosemary

peppercorns

For the accompaniment:

1 ⅔ cups (250 g) fava beans, shelled

5 green onions

1 clove garlic

4 Tbsp extra-virgin olive oil

salt and pepper

Chop the thyme, the chives, the rosemary, and the garlic, and place them in a bowl along with the peppercorns and the oil. Marinate the tuna in this mixture for approximately two hours in the refrigerator, covered with plastic wrap.

1. Cut the green onions into rounds and simmer them over low heat in a pan with a small amount of extra-virgin olive oil (add a bit of water if necessary).

2. Shell the fava beans and toss them in a pan with the oil and one clove of garlic, smashed (Picture 1). Season with salt and pepper.

3. Coat the tuna with the marinade (Picture 2) and scald in a pan for thirty seconds on each side (Picture 3).

4. Serve the fillet, sliced, over a bed of spring onions and accompanied by the fava beans.

Kitchen tip: Cut the tuna into long, narrow pieces. Brown in a pan with oil containing one clove of garlic and seasoned with a sprig of thyme (to be discarded after cooking). Salt and pepper and, as soon as the tuna turns color, set aside. Whip approximately ½ cup (60 g) of pitted Greek olives in a blender or food processor and spread over the tuna. Finely mince two red bell peppers, roasted and skinned, until they form a cream. Lightly season with salt and pepper. Slice the tuna and serve over the bell pepper cream.

Preparation time: 20 minutes
Cooking time: 10 minutes
Difficulty: Medium
Calories: 319
Wine: Alto Adige Chardonnay

Shrimp with Salama da Sugo, Melon,
and Gingered Yogurt

Serves 4

For the shrimp:
20 Shrimp
1 small melon
½ cup yogurt, plain
1 piece ginger root, fresh
mesclun
½ salama da sugo sausage, cooked
(flavorful Italian sausage)
fines herbs
4 Tbsp extra-virgin olive oil
salt and pepper

Preparation time: 30 minutes
Cooking time: 10 minutes
Difficulty: Medium
Calories: 605
Wine: Malvasia Istriana

Remove the rind from the melon and julienne. Julienne the salama da sugo sausage (Picture 1) as well.

1. Steam the shrimp, sprinkle with fines herbs (Picture 2), and dress them with extra-virgin olive oil, salt, and pepper.

2. Mix the yogurt with salt, pepper, grated ginger, and a small amount of olive oil (Picture 3).

3. Using a pasta cutter or similar tool, arrange the seasoned mesclun, the shrimp, the Salama da Sugo, and the melon on the serving plate (Picture 4). Dress with the yogurt sauce and serve.

Interesting to Know: salama da sugo is a culinary specialty of the Ferrara region of Italy. It is a kind of sausage made with high-quality pork mixed with red wine and natural spices and allowed to age from six months to a year. The preparation method is as follows: wrap the salama da sugo in a dish towel, suspend it from a stick or wooden spoon placed across the rim of a pot full of hot water (to make sure the Salama does not touch either the sides or the bottom of the pot), and boil for approximately six hours.

Salmon and Spinach
Mini-Tarts

Serves 4

For the puff pastry:
⅔ cup (80 g) all-purpose flour
3 Tbsp (40 ml) water
¾ stick (100 g) margarine
salt

For the tart filling:
¾ lb (350 g) salmon fillets
½ lb (250 g) spinach, fresh
1 egg
⅓ cup (100 ml) cream, fresh
1 shallot
2 Tbsp milk
salt and pepper

For the mousse:
⅓ cup (100 g) tomato sauce
⅔ cup (150 g) whipping cream, fresh
1 leaf gelatin
basil
salt and pepper

Preparation time: 40 minutes
Cooking time: 20 minutes
Difficulty: Medium
Calories: 544
Wine: Erbaluce di Caluso

Prepare the puff pastry dough according to directions provided on p. 10-11. Cut approximately ⅓ lb (150 g) of the salmon into small cubes. Finely mince the shallot and simmer with two tablespoons of water and a pinch of salt.

1. Cut the rest of the salmon into small pieces and pulse for a few seconds in a food processor. A little at a time, incorporate the shallot, the egg white (save the yolk), and the cream (which should be cold). Transfer the mixture to a bowl and add the previously cubed salmon. Adjust for salt and pepper and set aside. Wash and blanch the spinach for thirty seconds in boiling salted water. Drain and squeeze to remove any excess liquid.

2. Roll out the pastry dough and line four individual aluminium moulds (Picture 1). In the bottom of each, arrange a thin layer of spinach, fill with the salmon mixture, and cover with another layer of spinach (Picture 2). Finish with a disc of dough and seal the edges. Brush the tarts with egg yolk mixed with two tablespoons of milk. Bake in a preheated 400°F (200°C) oven for ten to fifteen minutes.

3. Soak the gelatin in cold water and squeeze to remove excess liquid. Heat the tomato sauce, add the gelatin, mix, and set aside to cool. Whip the cream, mix very gently with the tomato mixture (Picture 3), season with salt and pepper, and place in the refrigerator to set.

4. Serve the salmon and spinach mini-tarts warm with a dollop of tomato mousse.

1

2

3

Octopus with Zucchini
and Fine Herbs

Serves 4

For the octopus:
1 ¾ lb (800 g) octopus
1 small onion
1 small piece of celery
3 carrots

For the herb dressing:
1 sprig chives
5-6 basil leaves
3-4 sprigs thyme
½ lemon
4 Tbsp extra-virgin olive oil
salt and pepper

For the zucchini:
1 clove garlic
¾ lb (400 g) zucchini
⅓ lb (150 g) tomatoes, round
1 tsp extra-virgin olive oil
2 sprigs thyme
salt and pepper

Preparation time: 40 minutes
Cooking time: 1 hour
Difficulty: Easy
Calories: 272
Wine: Vermentino della Riviera
Ligure di Ponente

Peel the onion and cut into small pieces. Clean the celery, peel the carrot, and cut both into matchsticks. Place the onion, the celery, and the carrot into a pot of boiling salted water. Add the octopus and cook for forty to fifty minutes. Drain the octopus, cool by passing under running water, remove the skin, and cut into medium-large rings.

1. Prepare the herb dressing: Mince the thyme, the chives, and the basil. Squeeze the juice of ½ lemon into a bowl, add the minced herbs, salt, and pepper. Blend well and pour over the octopus (Picture 1). Cover with plastic wrap and set aside.

2. Wash the zucchini, cut lengthwise, and eliminate the white portion of the interior. Cut the green portion into strips and then into cubes. Blanch the tomatoes in boiling water for two minutes, peel and cube, and set aside.

3. Brown the clove of garlic in a pan, add the zucchini, the chopped thyme (Picture 2), salt, and pepper and cook over high heat for five minutes.

4. Distribute the zucchini onto serving plates, spoon two tablespoons of herbed octopus and the cubed tomatoes onto the plates, and serve.

Beet Salad
with Grilled Scallops

Serves 4

For the salad:

2 medium-large potatoes, yellow

2 red beets, cooked and vacuum-packed

4 large, fresh scallops

6 Tbsp extra-virgin olive oil

powdered seafood seasoning

1 bunch wild arugula

½ lemon

pine nuts

salt and pepper

Preparation time: 15 minutes
Cooking time: 30 minutes
Difficulty: Easy
Calories: 234
Wine: Alto Adige Pinot Bianco

Place the potatoes in cold salted water and bring to a boil. Cook until they are tender in the center. As soon as they have cooled, peel them and cut them into slices along with the beets (Picture 1). Arrange the potatoes and beets on plates in a crown shape.

1. Toast the pine nuts in a frying pan. Dress the scallops with the seafood seasoning and roast them in a non-stick pan with a drizzle of oil (Picture 2).

2. Chop the arugula (Picture 3) and dress with oil, salt, pepper, and lemon juice.

3. Arrange the scallops at the center of the potatoes and beets and surround them with the arugula and the toasted pine nuts. Dress with salt, pepper, and oil and serve.

Kitchen tip: Try scalding the scallops in a pan in which you have previously tossed ⅔ lb (300 g) of zucchini cut into small cubes, two tablespoons of oil, and a clove of garlic. Add salt and pepper and arrange the scallops in their shells. Top with about 2 slices of bread whipped in a food processor with parsley leaves and two tablespoons of oil. Crust in the oven for ten minutes at 400°F (200°C). Finish with a sauce made of approximately ⅓ cup (100 ml) of fresh cream, ¼ cup of white wine, about ¾ cup (200 ml) of vegetable broth, ginger, salt, and pepper. Bring the sauce to a boil, cook until reduced by half, filter, and whip in a food processor for a few seconds.

Marinated Scallops Mille Feuille
with Swiss Chard and Potato Purée

Serves 4

For the mille feuille:

10 scallops

1 small bunch Swiss chard

3 potatoes, medium

1 whole coconut

extra-virgin olive oil

salt

white pepper

Garnish:

shaved coconut meat

1 tomato

chervil

Preparation time: 45 minutes
Cooking time: 6 minutes
Difficulty: Easy
Calories: 442
Wine: Malvasia Istriana

Break open the coconut. Using a corkscrew, make a small hole in one of the three round indentations at one end of the coconut. Save the coconut water and open the nut.

1. Clean the scallops thoroughly, being sure to remove any sand. Divide them in half (Picture 1) and place them in a container that will allow them to be covered completely with the coconut water (Picture 2). Marinate for approximately five hours.

2. Clean the chard, cut it into small pieces, and cook in a small amount of lightly salted water. Drain and sauté for a few minutes in a drizzle of olive oil.

3. Boil and peel the potatoes. Mash them with a potato masher or ricer, and place into a pastry bag.

4. Prepare a stainless-steel cake pan or baking disc lined with parchment or non-stick oven paper and fill it, alternating the potatoes with the simmered chard and the scallops (Picture 3).

5. Bake for six minutes at 400°F (210°C). Transfer to a plate and garnish with shredded coconut, tomato, and chervil, according to taste.

Interesting to Know: The bitter note of the Swiss chard provides a pleasant contrast to the rest of the ingredients, enhancing the sweet, delicate flavor of the scallops.

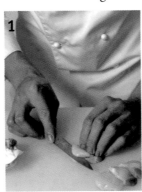

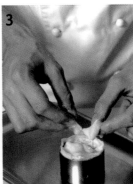

Black-Eyed Peas
with Baby Squid

Serves 4

For the black-eyed peas:

1 cup (200 g) black-eyed peas

⅓ lb (130 g) baby squid

2 cloves garlic

4 Tbsp extra-virgin olive oil

1 sprig rosemary

6 cherry tomatoes

parsley

seasoned salt for seafood

salt and pepper

Cook the black-eyed peas (which have been soaked overnight) in a pressure cooker, if possible, with salted water, a clove of garlic (unpeeled), and the sprig of rosemary.

1. Wash the squid, which should be as fresh as possible, removing the eyes and the cartilaginous pen that runs along the back.

2. Brown the remaining clove of garlic in a pan with a small amount of oil and the tomatoes, thoroughly washed and cut in two.

3. Season with salt and pepper and, shortly afterward, add the drained black-eyed peas. Add a small amount of hot water and let the flavors blend.

4. Distribute the piping hot black-eyed peas on four small trays. Dust the squid with the seasoned salt and roast them for a few seconds in a dry, non-stick pan. Drizzle with cold-pressed extra-virgin olive oil.

Kitchen tip: In place of the baby squid, you can substitute the small octopus known in Italy as moscardini. In that case, follow the recipe above, cleaning and slicing the octopus (Picture 1) and roasting it in a small amount of oil and seasoned seafood salt (Picture 2). Moscardini come in essentially two varieties—the first is called the moscardino muschiato (literally the "musky octopus") while the more highly prized is the so-called white moscardino, which has a milder flavor but is very tasty when fried.

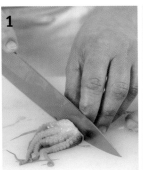
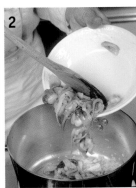

Preparation time: 15 minutes
Cooking time: 35 minutes
Difficulty: Easy
Calories: 254
Wine: Ribolla Gialla

Shrimp Salad with Cannellini Beans
and Crunchy Green Onions

Serves 4

For the salad:
1 cup (200 g) cannellini beans
⅓ cup (100 ml) white vinegar
3 Tbsp extra-virgin olive oil
12 large shrimp tails
1 bay leaf
1 sprig tarragon, fresh
a pinch sugar
salt and pepper

For the Green onions:
2 green onions
1 tsp all-purpose flour

For frying:
peanut oil

Soak the cannellini beans overnight in cold water. Boil them for thirty-five to forty minutes in a sauce pan with salted water and the bay leaf.

1. Boil the vinegar with a pinch of sugar in a small sauce pan and reduce to half its volume. Remove from heat and add the chopped tarragon.

2. Cut the green onions lengthwise into thin slices (Picture 1), dredge lightly in flour, and fry for a few minutes in hot oil. Drain them on paper towels.

3. Drain the beans and, while they are still warm, dress them with the olive oil, the tarragon-flavored vinegar, salt, and pepper.

4. Shell the shrimp, leaving a bit of shell at the end of the tail. Eliminate the black thread using a toothpick (Picture 2). In a third sauce pan, boil the shrimp in salted water for three minutes. Drain the shrimp tails well.

5. Arrange the cannellini beans in the center of a serving dish. Lay the shrimp tails and the rings of fried spring onion over the beans. Sprinkle, according to taste, with a bit of chopped tarragon. Serve slightly warm.

Preparation time: 20 minutes
Cooking time: 1 hour
Difficulty: Medium
Calories: 392
Wine: Colli di Luni Vermentino

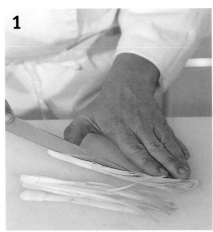

Grilled Sardines with Fried Potatoes
and Fennel Purée

Serves 4

For the sardines:
12 sardines
3 large potatoes
4 cups (1 lt) oil, for frying

For the fennel purée:
1 fennel bulb
1 potato
1 shallot
2 Tbsp extra-virgin olive oil
salt and pepper

For the marinade:
1 lemon
1 tbsp Peppercorns
1 small sprig wild fennel
3 Tbsp extra-virgin olive oil

Garnish:
⅕ lb (100 g) lettuce
wild fennel

Preparation time: 30 minutes
Cooking time: 35 minutes
Difficulty: Easy
Calories: 460
Wine: Cinque Terre Bianco

Clean the sardines (Pictures 1-2), open each like a book, wash, and dry them on absorbent paper towels.

1. Mix the lemon juice with the peppercorns, the olive oil, and the finely chopped wild fennel to create a marinade. Pour the marinade over the sardines and allow them to stand for twenty minutes (Picture 3).

2. Sauté the chopped shallot in a sauce pan with a tablespoon of olive oil. Add the fennel bulb and the potato cut into pieces. Cover with a small amount of water, add salt, and cook for approximately twenty-five minutes. In a food processor, whip the ingredients together with the rest of the olive oil and season with pepper. Keep the fennel purée warm while you prepare the potatoes and the sardines.

3. Peel the potatoes, slice them thinly (Picture 4), and place them in a bowl with cold water. Drain and dry well. Heat the oil in a pan and fry the potatoes. Drain on absorbent paper towels.

4. Scald the sardines for two minutes per side on a hot grill. Distribute the purée on the serving plate and arrange the sardines and fried potatoes around it. Garnish with chopped wild fennel. If desired, accompany the plate with a side-salad of lettuce.

Zucchini Stuffed
with Salmon and Caprino Cheese

Serves 4

For the zucchini:
8 large zucchini
½ lb (200 g) smoked salmon
⅔ cup (150 g) ricotta, fresh
½ cup (100 g) caprino cheese
2 Tbsp fresh cream
1 Tbsp extra-virgin olive oil
thyme
chives
salt and pepper

Preparation time: 20 minutes
Cooking time: 10 minutes
Difficulty: Easy
Calories: 308
Wine: Greco di Tufo

Wash the zucchini and remove both ends. Cut in half lengthwise, salt lightly, and place in a vegetable steamer or basket. Steam, inside a large, covered saucepan with a small amount of water (Picture 1), for ten minutes.

1. Allow the zucchini to cool and hollow them out with a teaspoon or a small melon baller (Picture 2).

2. Cut the salmon into small pieces and place in a blender or food processor with the caprino cheese, the ricotta, the fresh cream, the extra-virgin olive oil, a pinch of salt, and a bit of pepper. Pulse the ingredients together to create a cream and pour into a bowl.

3. Mince the chives and the thyme and incorporate into the mousse (Picture 3). Taste and adjust flavors. Turn the mousse into a pastry bag and fill the barely cooled zucchini halves (Picture 4).

4. You can serve immediately, while the zucchini is still warm, or you can place them in the refrigerator to chill and serve later.

Kitchen tip: For a filling with a more decisive taste, add two drops of Tabasco sauce to the mousse along with the herbs.

Sandwich Loaf with Salmon
and Cream Cheese Filling

Serves 6-8

For the sandwich filling:
1 entire loaf bread
1 lb (400 g) smoked salmon
¾ cup (200 g) cream cheese
nutmeg
salt and pepper

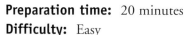

Preparation time: 20 minutes
Difficulty: Easy
Calories: 392
Wine: Prosecco di Valdobbiadene

Cut the bread so as to remove the center intact, leaving the crust (Picture 1), which you will use later.

1. Mix the cheese together with the nutmeg, the salt, and the pepper. Blend in a bowl. Slice the center of the bread into squares and spread them with the cheese mixture. (Picture 2).

2. Create sandwiches with the bread squares, using the sliced salmon (Picture 3). Cut them into four smaller squares and reform the bread loaf (Picture 4).

3. Serve the sandwich loaf as an appetizer.

Kitchen tip: Use your favorite fresh, spreadable cheese for this recipe. Start with the more common varieties, available in any supermarket, and build up to cheeses with more distinctive and unique flavors.

Lobster and Fennel Salad
with Orange Mayonnaise

Serves 6

For the salad:
3 whole lobsters (1 - 1 ¼ lb or 500-600 g each)
3 fennel bulbs

For the court-bouillon:
1 carrot
1 stalk celery
½ onion
1 bay leaf
3 Tbsp vinegar
8 cups (2 lt) water
salt

For the mayonnaise:
1 ⅓ cups (350 ml) peanut oil
3 eggs
½ orange
½ lemon
salt and pepper

For the dressing:
¾ cup (100 g) taggiasca olives, pitted
4 Tbsp extra-virgin olive oil
1 small bunch dill
½ lemon
salt

Preparation time: 30 minutes
Cooking time: 25 minutes
Difficulty: Medium
Calories: 670
Wine: San Severo Bianco

Bring the water to a boil with the vege es, the bay leaf, the vinegar, and the salt. Immerse the w e lobsters and cook for ten minutes. Drain the lobsters and run them under cold water to make them easier to shell (Picture 1).

1. Grate the orange peel (Picture 2) and squeeze, reserving the juice. Using a whisk, beat the egg yolks, the lemon juice, the juice obtained from the orange peel, and the salt in a mixing bowl. Drizzle the oil into the mixture, continuing to beat with the whisk. Add the grated orange peel and adjust for salt and pepper.

2. Cut the fennel into thin slices, blanch for three minutes in boiling salted water, set aside to cool, and dress with the lemon juice, oil, salt, and chopped dill.

3. Cut the lobsters into medallions and place on a serving platter with the fennel (use the fennel as a bed, or lay the lobster and fennel slices side by side) and the orange mayonnaise. Garnish with the olives and extra-virgin olive oil.

Interesting to Know: The French term, court-bouillon (which means "short broth"), indicates a spiced broth used for boiling fish.

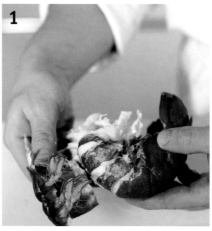

Octopus with Colorful
Vegetable Sauté

Serves 6

For the octopus:

2 ¼ lb (1 Kg) octopus

1 small stalk celery

1 lemon

½ onion

sea salt

For the vegetables:

¼ lb (100 g) carrots

⅓ lb (150 g) zucchini

⅓ lb (150 g) cherry tomatoes

2 artichokes

1 small red onion

1 clove garlic

1 Tbsp parsley

½ lemon

6 Tbsp extra-virgin olive oil

4-5 basil leaves

salt and pepper

Preparation time: 20 minutes
Cooking time: 50 minutes
Difficulty: Easy
Calories: 292
Wine: Riviera Ligure di Ponente
Pigato

Heat a pot containing heavily salted water. Add the celery, cleaned and cut into pieces, the lemon, and the coarsely sliced onion.

1. Boil the octopus for approximately forty minutes. Remove from heat and allow to cool in its cooking liquid. Drain the octopus well, remove skin, and slice into small rings. Place the octopus in a bowl and set aside.

2. Peel the carrots and the red onion. Eliminate the tough outer leaves of the artichokes.

3. Cut the cherry tomatoes into wedges (Picture 1) and place them in a bowl. Cut the carrots and the zucchini into matchsticks and slice the artichoke thinly.

4. Dress the octopus with salt, pepper, and the juice of one-half lemon. Add to the vegetables fresh from the sauté pan and serve immediately.

1

2

Shrimp in Zucchini
Roll-Ups

Serves 4

For the roll-ups:
⅓ lb (200 g) zucchini
¾ lb (400 g) shrimp
4 sprigs lemon thyme
⅔ lb (250 g) cherry tomatoes
1 medium leek
4 Tbsp extra-virgin olive oil
salt and pepper

Preparation time: 30 minutes
Cooking time: 15 minutes
Difficulty: Easy
Calories: 156
Wine: Alto Adige Gewürztraminer

Clean the zucchini, and remove the ends. Then using an electric slicer or a sharp knife, slice the zucchini very thinly lengthwise.

1. Bring water to a boil in a sauce pan and salt lightly. Boil the sliced zucchini in the water for one minute, drain, and set aside to cool.

2. Clean and peel the shrimp. Heat the olive oil in a pan. When the oil is hot, brown the shrimp thoroughly (Picture 1). Adjust for salt and pepper. When the shrimp are cooked through, arrange them on a tray.

3. Wash the cherry tomatoes and cut them in half. Remove the thyme leaves from their sprigs. Clean the leeks, cut them into rounds, and brown them in the pan in which the shrimp were cooked (Picture 2). Add the cherry tomatoes (Picture 3) and thyme leaves. Season with salt and pepper.

4. Lay out the zucchini slices and place a shrimp across each one. Wrap the zucchini around the shrimp (Picture 4).

5. Distribute one tablespoon each of leeks and cherry tomatoes on serving plates. Add the zucchini and shrimp roll-ups. Season with salt and pepper, drizzle with olive oil, and serve.

Squid and Shrimp
in Orange and Ginger Dressing

Serves 4

For the seafood:
⅔ lb (320 g) squid
⅓ lb (130 g) shrimp
1 bay leaf
1 small stalk celery
¼ shallot
½ Tbsp cumin seeds
salt

For the dressing:
½ lb (240 g) oranges
1 small piece ginger root
3 Tbsp extra-virgin olive oil
1 lemon
1 orange
chives
salt and pepper

Place the celery and the shallot (cut into small pieces), the bay leaf, and the cumin into a pot of boiling water. Add salt and allow to simmer over low heat.

1. Wash the squid, eliminating the internal organs. Shell the shrimp, wash them, and set aside on a plate. Boil the squid for five to six minutes in the pot containing the vegetables. Drain and place in a bowl. Cook the shrimp in the same liquid for two minutes. Drain and add to the squid.

2. Peel the oranges. As you are peeling, conserve the juice in a cup and add the juice of half a lemon.

3. Peel the ginger and cut into thin strips. Brown the ginger in a small pan with two tablespoons of oil. When the ginger begins to brown, add the orange and lemon juice. Remove from heat and pour the mixture into a large bowl. Add the orange wedges, the rest of the oil, and the chives and season lightly with salt and pepper, mixing well.

4. Arrange the squid and the shrimp on individual serving plates and dress with the orange and ginger sauce (Picture 1).

Preparation time: 35 minutes
Cooking time: 12 minutes
Difficulty: Medium
Calories: 146
Wine: Trentino Müller Thurgau

Savory Tomato
and Sardine Pie

Serves 6

For the crust:
¾ lb (400 g) bread dough
4 Tbsp extra-virgin olive oil

For the filling:
1 lb (500 g) Tomatoes, ripe
1 onion
4 Tbsp extra-virgin olive oil
⅔ lb (300 g) sardines, salt-packed
⅕ lb (100 g) caciocavallo cheese
salt and pepper

Preparation time: 35 minutes
Cooking time: 30 minutes
Difficulty: Easy
Calories: 520
Wine: Fiano di Avellino

On a bread board or other suitable surface, knead the bread dough with the olive oil (Picture 1). Wash the tomatoes and blanch in boiling water for thirty seconds. Peel, remove seeds, and chop.

1. In a pan, sauté the chopped onion with the olive oil. As soon as the onion begins to turn a golden color, add the tomatoes (Picture 2). Season lightly with salt and pepper and cook over low heat for twenty to twenty-five minutes.

2. Wash the sardines, eliminate the heads, and add half of them to the tomato mixture (Picture 3), flavoring them for approximately ten minutes.

3. Line an oiled 9-10 inch baking dish with the dough and pour half of the sardine and tomato mixture, along with the caciocavallo cut into small cubes, over the dough. Bake at 350°F (180°C) for twenty minutes.

4. Remove the pie from the oven, cover with the rest of the sardine and tomato sauce, and distribute the remaining sardines over the surface (Picture 4). Drizzle with oil and bake for another ten minutes. Remove from the oven and serve immediately.

Stuffed Squid
with Fresh Tomato

Serves 6

For the squid:
2 large squid (approx. 1 ¼ lb or 600g each)
½ onion
2 Tbsp extra-virgin olive oil
¼ cup white wine

For the filling:
1 ½ (300 g) cups peas
½ onion
⅓ cup (100 g) ricotta
8 Tbsp bread crumbs
2 Tbsp extra-virgin olive oil
2 Tbsp parmesan cheese
salt and pepper

For the tomatoes:
3 tomatoes, vine-ripened
1 small bunch chives
2 Tbsp extra-virgin olive oil
salt and pepper

Preparation time: 25 minutes
Cooking time: 40 minutes
Difficulty: Easy
Calories: 390
Wine: Lugana

Mince the onion. Sauté one half in two tablespoons olive oil. Add the peas. Season with salt and add ¼ cup of water. Cook, covered, for fifteen to twenty minutes.

1. Mash the peas with a ricer or potato masher and place the resulting purée in a bowl. Set aside to cool, then add the ricotta, the bread crumbs, and the cheese. Adjust for salt and pepper.

2. Clean the squid (Picture 1). Wash and dry them, then stuff with the pea mixture. Close each squid with a toothpick (Picture 2).

3. Sauté the rest of the onion in two tablespoons of oil. Brown the squid, add the white wine, and allow it to evaporate. Cook, covered, for fifteen to twenty minutes, adding a small amount of water if needed.

4. Blanch the tomatoes in boiling water for thirty seconds. Peel them, eliminate the seeds, and cut into small cubes. Dress them with the remaining olive oil, the salt, the pepper, and the julienned chives. Add the chopped tomato to the squid and let the flavors merge for two minutes. Cut the squid into rings and serve, accompanied by its cooking liquid.

1

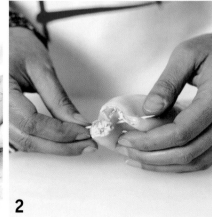
2

Tuna Pâté
with Marsala Cream

Serves 4

For the pâté:

1 can (160 g) Tuna, oil-packed
¾ stick (100 g) butter
1 egg yolk
1 tsp anchovy paste
1 cube instant gelatin
1 Tbsp balsamic vinegar
4 cucumber pickles
8 slices white sandwich bread
¼ cup Marsala wine, dry
2 cups (500 ml) water

Preparation time: 15 minutes
Cooking time: 5 minutes
Difficulty: Easy
Calories: 363
Wine: Verduzzo di Ramandolo

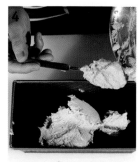

Prepare the gelatin: Melt the gelatin in 2 cups (500 ml) of water over medium heat. Remove the sauce pan from the heat and add the balsamic vinegar (Picture 1). Mix the gelatin and pour a layer into the bottom of a non-stick mold. Place in the refrigerator to harden.

1. Cut the pickles into small slices and arrange over the hardened gelatin.

2. Using a blender or food processor, whip together the tuna, the butter, the anchovy paste, the egg yolk, and the wine (Pictures 2-3). Pour part of the resulting cream over the solidified gelatin (Picture 4) and allow to harden in the refrigerator.

3. When the gelatin mixture appears to be sufficiently solid, remove the mold from the refrigerator and add another layer of gelatin and of tuna cream. Return the pâté to the refrigerator and allow to harden for at least two hours.

4. Ten minutes before serving, remove the pâté from the refrigerator. Place the mold in hot water for a moment and then unmould the pâté. Cut the bread cross-wise to create triangles and remove the crust. Toast lightly and serve with the pâté.

Gilthead Carpaccio on Potato Wafers
with Baby Spinach

Serves 4

For the carpaccio:
½ lb (200 g) gilthead seabream,
   fillets

For the dressing
6 Tbsp extra-virgin olive oil
1 tsp cumin
1 lemon
salt and pepper

For the potato wafers:
2 (350 g) large potatoes
4 Tbsp extra-virgin olive oil
¼ lb (100 g) baby spinach
salt and pepper

Preparation time: 20 minutes
Cooking time: 15 minutes
Difficulty: Easy
Calories: 299
Wine: Dolcetto di Diano d'Alba

Peel the potatoes and grate them into a mixing bowl (or use a food processor).

1. Grease a non-stick pan with one tablespoon of oil, pour half of the grated potatoes into the centre of the pan (Picture 1) and, using your hands, spread them out to form a disc (Picture 2). Cook the grated potatoes over medium heat for two to three minutes on each side. Cook the other half of the potatoes in the same way.

2. Lay the discs on your work surface and, using a biscuit cutter or similar device, cut out small circles about 2-½ to 2-¾ inches (6-7 cm) in diameter (Picture 3). The potatoes should yield approximately twelve discs in all. Arrange the discs on a greased baking sheet and bake at 350°F (180°C) for approximately ten minutes or until they are crunchy.

3. Squeeze the lemon into a mixing bowl, add the ground cumin, the oil, salt, and pepper and mix until the vinaigrette emulsifies.

4. Cut the seabream fillet to create a number of very thin slices (Picture 4). Arrange them on a tray, dress with the vinaigrette, and marinate for five minutes.

5. When the potato wafers are cooked, arrange them on serving plates and place a few slices of seabream carpaccio over each. Alongside, place baby spinach leaves seasoned with oil and salt. Serve immediately.

Spinach and Shrimp Pockets
with Ricotta Cheese

Serves 4

For the dough:
1 ½ cups (200 g) all-purpose flour
½ cup (100 g) cow's milk ricotta, fresh
3 pats butter
salt

For the filling:
1 lb (400 g) spinach
¾ lb (300 g) shrimp
1 pat butter
¼ cup milk
1 bay leaf
salt and pepper

Quickly blend the ingredients for the dough to obtain a stiff, smooth mixture. Place into a floured bowl, cover with plastic wrap, and let stand in the refrigerator for thirty minutes.

1. Clean the spinach and the shrimp. Boil the shrimp for five to ten minutes. Drain and allow them to cool.

2. Dissolve the butter in a non-stick pan with one bay leaf and add the shrimp (Picture 1). Allow the flavors to blend for five minutes. Add the spinach and the milk (Picture 2) and adjust for salt and pepper. Let the liquids evaporate, then set aside to cool.

3. Remove the chilled dough from the refrigerator and extend with a rolling pin to a thickness of just under ½ inch (1 cm). Flour the rim of a glass and use it as a dough cutter in order to create discs. Place one tablespoon of filling on each. Fold the disc over to create a half-moon shape (Picture 3) and seal carefully, pressing with the fingers.

4. Cover a cookie sheet with parchment or non-stick oven paper. Arrange the pockets on the sheet, brush them with cold milk, and place in a preheated 350°F (180°C) oven for approximately thirty minutes. Remove from the oven when they are golden-brown and serve immediately.

Preparation time: 30 minutes
Cooking time: 30 minutes
Difficulty: Easy
Calories: 394
Wine: Capri Bianco

Shrimp Mini-Quiches

Serves 6

For the shortcrust pastry:
2 ⅓ cups (300 g) all-purpose flour
1 Tbsp extra-virgin olive oil
2 Tbsp white wine
1 ⅓ stick (150 g) butter
1 whole egg, plus 1 egg yolk
salt

For the filling:
⅔ lb (300 g) shrimp
¾ lb (320 g) red radicchio
1 Tbsp parsley
3 Tbsp cream
1 Tbsp white wine
1 egg
2 Tbsp extra-virgin olive oil
salt and pepper

Pour the flour into a bowl, add the butter softened at room temperature, the salt, the white wine, the whole egg, and the egg yolk. Finally, add the olive oil and mix together quickly to blend the ingredients well.

1. Place the dough in a plastic bag and let stand in the refrigerator for twenty minutes. Clean the radicchio and discard the white center rib in each leaf. Cut the red portion of the leaf into thin strips.

2. Brown the radicchio in a sauté pan with the oil and the chopped parsley. Lightly season with salt and pepper. After a few minutes, add the wine. When it has evaporated, add the cream, mix, and allow to thicken. Break the remaining egg into the sauté pan, remove from heat, and mix rapidly.

3. Place the brisée dough on your work surface. Roll out the dough with a rolling pin to a thickness of approximately 1/4 inch (1/2 cm). Butter and flour small baking tins or ramekins and line them with the dough (Picture 1). In each, arrange the already-cleaned shrimp (Picture 2), then fill with the sautéed radicchio and its cooking liquid (Picture 3). Bake at 350°F (170°C) for twenty-five minutes. Serve warm.

Preparation time: 25 minutes
Cooking time: 35 minutes
Difficulty: Medium
Calories: 549
Wine: Alto Adige Gewürztraminer

1 2 3

Fried Mini-Pizzas
with Clams and Fresh Tomato

Serves 4

For the dough:
2 ½ cups (350 g) all-purpose flour
1 egg
½ packet brewer's yeast
½ cup (120 ml) water
2 Tbsp extra-virgin olive oil
⅓ cup (100 ml) peanut oil
salt

For the clams:
2 ½ lb (1 Kg) clams
1 clove garlic
1 bunch parsley
4-5 basil leaves
1 lb (400 g) tomatoes, round
6 Tbsp extra-virgin olive oil
salt and pepper

Preparation time: 25 minutes
Cooking time: 25 minutes
Difficulty: Easy
Calories: 612
Wine: Falerno dei Colli Ascolani

Mix together all the ingredients for the dough. Work the dough until it is smooth and soft. Cover the container with plastic wrap and allow the dough to rise for approximately one hour.

1. Wash the clams and place them in a pan with the parsley, the garlic, and two tablespoons of oil. Cover and cook for five minutes until the shells are completely open. Drain and discard any clams that have remained closed. Extract the meat from the remaining shells.

2. Blanch the tomatoes for a few seconds in boiling water, peel, eliminate the seeds, and cut into cubes. Heat the rest of the oil in a separate sauté pan. Add the cubed tomatoes, the clams, and the chopped basil. Lightly season with salt and pepper and toss for two minutes (Picture 1).

3. Roll out the dough for the mini-pizzas to a thickness of approximately ¼ inch (½ cm) and use a circular biscuit cutter or similar tool to cut out discs (Picture 2). Heat the oil in a non-stick pan, fry one mini-pizza at a time for two to three minutes on each side (Pictures 3-4) and drain on a paper towel. Fry all of the discs and keep them warm (for example, in the oven set to a low temperature).

4. Place the pizza discs on plates and distribute the clam and tomato mixture over each before serving.

Salmon Tartare
in Vodka Sauce

Serves 4

For the tartare:

¾ lb (400 g) salmon, fresh
½ cup vodka
1 bunch arugula
2 egg yolks
3 Tbsp extra-virgin olive oil
1 tsp mustard
1 lemon
⅔ cup (150 ml) sunflower or other light vegetable oil
1 sprig chives
salt and pepper

Garnish:

4 radishes
a small bunch of lettuce leaves

Place the egg yolks in a mixing bowl with the mustard, the juice of half a lemon, and one tablespoon of oil. Begin beating with a whisk, drizzling in additional oil (Picture 1) in order to obtain a thick, dense mayonnaise. Add salt and the julienned chives.

1. Remove any bones from the salmon and discard the skin. Chop the meat with a knife (Picture 2) and transfer to a mixing bowl. Dress with two tablespoons extra-virgin olive oil, salt, pepper, the juice of half a lemon, and a dash of vodka.

2. Wash and chop the arugula and add it to the salmon. Allow the tartare to take on flavour for a few minutes, then serve with the chive mayonnaise, a few leaves of lettuce, and the radishes.

Kitchen tip: If you would prefer not to use vodka, grate approx. 3 Tbsp (50 g) of fresh ginger root, squeeze the resulting pulp, and add the juice to the oil and lemon juice marinade.

Preparation time: 30 minutes
Difficulty: Easy
Calories: 517
Wine: Pinot Grigio

Tuna Loaf

Serves 4

For the loaf:

1 ½ cans (250 g) tuna, oil-packed

4 anchovies, salt-preserved

2 eggs

1 bunch parsley

4 Tbsp bread crumbs

salt and pepper

For the sauce:

2 anchovies

1 Tbsp capers, salt-preserved

2 Tbsp extra-virgin olive oil

1 tsp vinegar

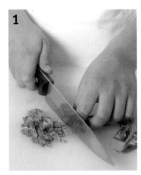

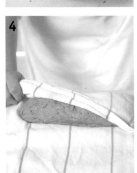

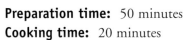

Preparation time: 50 minutes
Cooking time: 20 minutes
Difficulty: Easy
Calories: 360
Wine: Lamezia Bianco

Drain the tuna and break apart with a fork. Rinse the anchovies under running water to remove salt, eliminate the bones, and cut into small pieces (Picture 1). Wash the parsley and chop finely.

1. In a mixing bowl, place the well separated tuna, the anchovies, and the chopped parsley (Picture 2). Mix well and add salt and pepper to taste. Blend in the bread crumbs (Picture 3) and bind with the eggs, stirring to produce an even mixture.

2. Using your hands, shape the tuna loaf into a salami shape and wrap it in a clean dish cloth (Picture 4). Tie with kitchen string and transfer to a fish kettle or casserole dish of appropriate size.

3. Cover the loaf with cold water and cook for approximately twenty minutes from the moment when the water begins to boil. When cooking is complete, drain carefully and allow to cool before removing the dish cloth.

4. Prepare the sauce: Mix the capers (carefully rinsed of salt), the anchovies (deboned and chopped), the vinegar, and the oil.

5. Cut the tuna loaf into slices, arrange the slices on a serving dish, and serve accompanied by the caper sauce.